PRAISE FOR SOLO

"In its bravery, authenticity, and generosity, this book is pure gold. Through an honest reckoning of her own life, and the hard-won healing she co-created with the natural world, Glenda Goodrich suggests that we too might be capable of the extraordinary spiritual growth—the forgiveness, possibility, and redemption—described so beautifully in this book."
—Ellen Santasiero, Writing Coach and Editor; Co-editor
of *PLACED: An Encyclopedia of Central Oregon*

"A thrilling spiritual adventure that explores thirteen wilderness quests and thirteen life-changing questions. Goodrich takes readers through a world of vivid, gorgeously wrought landscapes, from the searing heat of Death Valley to the mossy rainforests of the North Cascades. A book for everyone who loves wild places and longs to live an examined life, *Solo Passage* is a wise, stunningly beautiful page-turner that will leave you moved, inspired and ready to connect more deeply with nature—and yourself."
—Rebecca Jamieson, author of *The Body of All Things*

"Inspired by the raw honesty of the wild, Glenda Goodrich's book is a unique memoir in that it invites the reader to accompany her on this journey and not simply witness it. Page after page, we are reminded that courage is not synonymous with fearlessness, and the quest is not a destination but an entry into an ongoing way of being. Take note readers, this book will draw you into your own vision quest. The author's willingness to reveal her struggle will compel you to examine your own life and question old feelings, false narratives and outdated identity structures. If you allow the wonder of these pages in, you will be transformed along the way."
—Philip Kenney, author of *The Writer's Crucible:*
Meditations on Emotion, Being and Creativity

"What can an elusive coyote convey to a woman about her troubled relationship with her father? How does rebelling against the "right thing" on a wilderness journey lead to a startling sense of freedom? Glenda Goodrich heads boldly into wild places in search of answers to the kinds of gritty, nagging personal questions that vex many of us all our lives, then reveals the "answers" she's found . . . sometimes indirect and sometimes precisely aimed, often mysterious, and always profound."

—Trebbe Johnson, author of *Fierce Consciousness: Surviving the Sorrows of Earth and Self* and *Radical Joy for Hard Times*

"A compelling story, told with courage and deep vulnerability, by a woman who goes out onto the earth in a ceremonial way to heal herself and understand her place in this world. Glenda's story is a celebration of interconnectedness and belonging, a wild sacrament, a love song to Mother Earth. Through her stories, the reader is shown a path to transformation that anyone who is drawn to can follow. Glenda shows us the earth belongs to us all, and our souls know how to open to its beauty and wisdom."

—Sara Harris, Co-Founder of EarthWays LLC, Wilderness Rites of Passage Guide

"Glenda's honest memoir about her personal wilderness vision quests is a powerful statement about the relevance of this ancient form to those of us in modern life. Through the humble, intimate stories of her life, the vivid descriptions of the places she quested, and her beautiful artwork, I am reminded to keep finding ways to engage in this spiritual practice the rest of my own life. Thank you, Glenda, for this gift of inspiration."

—Ann Linnea, author of *Deep Water Passage, a Spiritual Quest at Midlife*

"Glenda Goodrich carries bare-bones survival gear, deep intention, and astonishing trust as she ventures year after year into the wilderness in search of a deeper knowing of herself. Her seamless stories about the old ways of solitude, fasting, and exposure are laced with tenacity, tenderness, and the unexpected gifts of wild nature."
—Susan Hagen, co-author of *Women at Ground Zero*

"An introspective, poignant personal narrative written with raw, animated honesty. This beautifully crafted book is drenched in wonder and wrapped with tenderness. It is a celebration of interconnectedness and belonging, a poetic love letter to nature."
—Savannah Tenderfoot, Sensitivity Reader and Editor, Salt & Sage Books

"Glenda Goodrich's mesmerizing memoir of her over twenty years of solo wilderness quests is an exhilarating and tender read. In moving and penetrating prose, she faces her fears, grief, regrets, even transgressions with the trees, rocks, and creatures as her companions. Supported by the wisdom of ancient traditions and able guides, she stunningly recreates her sacred ceremonies as she fully embraces her artist, wise woman self."
—Wendy Judith Cutler, co-author of
Writing Alone Together

"A rare piece of literature. Raw, poetic, haunting. Effortlessly weaving the landscape into her narrative. Through direct experience, Goodrich creates a powerful testament to the restorative powers of nature, and its ability to heal the soul. It just might change your life."
—Scott Stillman, author of *Wilderness,*
The Gateway To The Soul

SOLO PASSAGE

Solo Passage

13 Quests, 13 Questions

Glenda Goodrich

SHE WRITES PRESS

Published 2023
Printed in the United States of America
Print ISBN: 978-1-64742-551-7
E-ISBN: 978-1-64742-552-4
Library of Congress Control Number: 2023908851

For information, address:
She Writes Press
1569 Solano Ave #546
Berkeley, CA 94707

She Writes Press is a division of SparkPoint Studio, LLC.

Interior design by Tabitha Lahr

For my children: Bill and Susie;
my grandchildren: Megan, Thea, and Silas;
my great-grandchildren: Jack, Nora, Caroline, and Molly;
and all future generations.

In that insight of inter-being, it is possible to have real communication with the earth, which is the highest form of prayer. In that kind of relationship, you have enough love, strength, and awakening . . . to change your life.

—Thich Nhat Hanh

CHAPTERS

Author's Note

The wilderness quest, also called a vision quest or a vision fast, is an ancient pan-cultural initiation rite of passage that encourages an awakening of one's own indigenous wisdom, personal vision, and purpose on Earth. The essence of the quest is the act of seeking or pursuing something. We walk alone into the womb of Mother Earth and ask a question in search of guidance so that we may show up more fully and better care for ourselves, our families, and our communities. The thirteen wilderness quests I wrote about in this book all revolved around a central question, which has been highlighted to stand out in the text. These questions related to my specific personal experience but are also posed for the reader's consideration. For example, the question on my first quest was: *What healing gifts would nature bring me if I opened myself up to the possibilities?* Readers might ask themselves the same question as they imagine how their own lives might be deepened by time alone in nature.

INTRODUCTION

"Grandma, will you tell us a story?" Silas asked.

"Yeah, Grandma, tell us one of your stories," Thea said. "One you haven't told us before."

My grandchildren had already heard the ones about the visit from horses, close encounters with spiders and snakes, sneaky pack rats, and foxes screaming at night.

"How about the black hole in the forest? Have I told you that one before?"

"No," they chorused.

The three of us were cuddled, like birds in a nest, in Thea's bed. My grandchildren had claimed ownership of my body. I was their soft and round, not-so-firm, terra firma to sit on and snuggle against. Thea, age nine, and Silas, age six, looked like a female and male version of the same person who had the best features of both their parents—round heads with thick coffee-colored hair, nut-brown eyes, and slightly turned-up noses.

I put an arm around each of their shoulders. The kids were little furnaces, radiating energy and heat. A revolving nightlight on the bedside table threw white stars on the dark walls and ceiling, disappearing and reappearing in rhythmic cycles.

"Once upon a time there was a woman who went into the wilderness . . ."

Thea and Silas were among the few people who'd heard these stories, although they thought the woman was simply a character I had created. But these stories were true. I was the woman who spent days at a time alone in the wild, without food, surrounded by wild creatures. I had shared my wilderness quest stories with a small circle of my closest friends, but I wasn't comfortable talking about them with anyone else. I couldn't distill them into one- or two-sentence explanations without minimizing the depth of my experiences.

I learned about wilderness questing in 1996 when my older sister Lea gave me *The Book of the Vision Quest*, by Steven Foster and Meredith Little, along with other books about Native culture and Southwest design that she'd picked up from a yard sale. She knew I liked Southwest lore and art. The vision quest book happened to have been in the stack. Wilderness questing, also known as vision questing or vision fasting, is a centuries-old rite of passage intended to awaken personal vision and purpose. It is an act of courage and determination that involves solitude, fasting, and prayer. Jesus went into the desert for forty days. The Buddha sat under the bodhi tree and found spiritual enlightenment. Muhammad went into the cave on the mountain and received the Koran. And I, an ordinary, middle-aged, middle-class white woman, went into the wilderness again and again for over two decades—in California, Oregon, and Washington State, to places like Death Valley, the Inyo, the Modoc, the Cascade-Siskiyou National Monument, and the North Cascades.

Each time, I went into the wild looking for something specific and came out with an unexpected treasure.

I honor the people who have held this ceremony and passed the teachings on through the generations so that non-Native people like me could experience the power of questing in wild places. My people come from Britain, Ireland, France, and Germany. As far as I know, I am the only person in my family who has ever participated in a wilderness quest.

The way my wilderness guides have explained it to me, no one owns the ceremony of the quest, but we honor Native peoples who have carried this forward so non-Native peoples might rediscover their long-ago indigenous roots and customs. Cultures throughout history have practiced some version of fasting and isolation as a rite of passage. Most of us who take part in questing today have been called to the ceremony from somewhere deep in our DNA, beckoned by ancient and enduring memories of our connection to Mother Earth. We long to be held by her. We long to remember ourselves back to her.

When I first read *The Book of the Vision Quest*, I didn't imagine going on a quest myself, but the seed was planted. Years later, in search of an adventure to mark a milestone birthday, I came across a flyer on a bulletin board in a bookstore that read: "Wilderness Rites Women's Vision Quests in Death Valley." Without hesitation I wrote down the phone number and made the call.

I was pleased to discover that Anne Stine, wilderness quest guide and founder of Wilderness Rites, had learned the ceremony from Steven Foster and Meredith Little. I thought wilderness questing was only a Native American practice, but I learned from Anne that Steven and Meredith had researched Indigenous peoples from all around the world and discovered common themes in their rite-of-passage ceremonies: isolation, fasting, and exposure; as well as the three phases of a traditional quest ceremony: severance, threshold, and incorporation. These themes spoke to me, and I was hungry to learn more, so I bought and read a book that Meredith wrote after Steven died, *The School of Lost Borders, A Love Story*. In it she wrote, "In the early 1970s, the time was ripe for bringing earth-based wisdom back into our culture." She went on to tell the stories of the Native people who helped her and Steven develop their own questing knowledge. Sun Bear, an elder and prominent voice in the Ojibwa tribe, took them under his wing. Hyemeyohsts Storm, of Cheyenne, Sioux, Irish American, and German descent, heard about Steven and Meredith's work and told them, "What you're doing is important. You sit down here, and I'm going to teach you things you need to know."

Grandpa Raymond Stone, a Paiute elder, gave them permission to use the land around Big Pine, California, and taught them about the Indigenous ways of perceiving the world "like no one else." Meredith wrote, "Grandpa Raymond was the real thing. He was taught by his father, who had been taught by his father, a lineage of 'Indian doctors' who were guided by spirit. Grandpa Raymond told us, 'You do good work. You need to do that work for your people.'"

I had read about fly-by-night guides who used pageantry and hype to pull people in, but who lacked the depth and understanding it takes to "be guided by spirit," as Meredith described it. Anne Stine's twenty-five years of experience guiding quests, along with how she had learned the ceremony from those who had learned it directly from Native elders, resonated with me. I felt that she, too, was the real thing. I wanted to be a part of something that felt legitimate and had components from all over the world.

I went on my first wilderness quest when I turned fifty, a rite of passage to mark my half-century point. I thought I'd try it once, to see if I could fast for four days and nights alone in the wild. At the time, I had no idea that wilderness questing would become an annual event in my life, a sacred ritual that connected me to the land, wove me into nature's web, and transformed me from a woman who worked to please everyone else into a woman who forged her own path. This book traces that transformation.

———————

Snuggled with the kids in our downy nest, I continued the story.

"Once upon a time, there was a woman who went into the wilderness to find a new name. She loaded her backpack and headed out for the sacred mountain. She talked, sang, and slept with all of Earth's creatures: the rocks, the plants and trees, the winged ones, the four-legged, the many-legged, and even the no-legged that crawled with their bellies close to Earth. To find her new name, she had to die to her old self."

"Wait . . . what? She dies?" Thea's eyes shone brightly, a furrow between her brows.

"Well, no, she doesn't really die, sweetie," I said, rubbing her back lightly. "It's called a rite of passage, like when you graduated from preschool to elementary, and you left your baby self behind. That's why people go on wilderness quests; something they don't need or want any more goes away, and something new takes its place."

"Oh, good. I don't want her to die," she said.

I kissed Thea on the top of her head and continued with the story.

"The woman spent long dark nights hungry and alone on a mountain. Her empty tummy growled, and she cried all by herself in the dark, you see."

"Why was she hungry?" Silas asked.

I smoothed his damp hair. "Because remember, on a wilderness quest you don't eat. You only drink water. It's called fasting."

"I'm going on a wilderness quest when I'm eight," Silas said.

"I'll take you out when you're ready," I said, delighted by his enthusiasm. "Are you ready to get back to the story?"

The children nodded.

"Well, I told you the woman was alone, but that wasn't really true. She had company on that mountaintop. Can you guess who came to see her?"

"A frog," Silas said.

"A dragon," Thea added.

"It was a long black snake that slithered down the path in front of her; she just barely missed stepping on it."

"Ooooo," they said in unison.

"Also, a coyote that howled in the night, and birds that sang in the trees like a wild church choir. Then, guess what she found next? Not a wild creature, but a tree stump."

"A tree stump?" Silas asked.

"That's right, a plain old tree stump. And she looked in it, down a long black hole, like a tunnel with no end. She called a prayer out loud, 'Black hole, bring me a name I can call myself —a new name for a new self.'"

───────── ⌣ ─────────

I finished telling my grandchildren the tale of the black hole that night, the gift that the tree stump gave the woman and the magic she made from nothing but a black hole. But there were other stories I wasn't ready to tell them—stories about how the woman in the story grew up with an alcoholic father, got pregnant at sixteen, was divorced twice, and had brushes with death, and how I was the woman in the stories, the one who spent long nights alone in the wild terrified. I would tell them later, when they were old enough to understand why I had felt compelled to go into the wilderness to heal from the trauma of my old life.

My time in the wild helped me circle back to the events of my life and sort through them, find deeper meaning, and make peace with my past.

I write this book and share my art as a legacy for my children, grandchildren, and great-grandchildren, as a pathway for my loved ones to follow and find their way back to their connection with Mother Earth. Through these stories, they can know how one of their ancestors lived, what she loved, and how the seed of wilderness questing was planted in her, took root in her life, and changed how she lived.

I write this book as encouragement and inspiration for you too. In each of the thirteen questing chapters, I ask a question that arose for me during my journey. I have carried these questions into my life to help me incorporate the gifts I received from each of my quests. If some of these questions resonate with you, take them into your heart and out onto the land. May you go out into the wilderness, lose yourself, and find yourself there too.

BELONGING TO
THE LAND

Body of earth . . . Tell the story of pure
mirrors. The Creator has given you
this splendor. Why talk of anything else?
—Rumi

Unbuckling my hip strap, I twisted to balance the pack on my hip and lowered the bulky bundle to the ground. The size of a small child, the pack held everything I'd need for my stay in Death Valley: sleeping bag, sleeping pad that folded into a camp chair, flashlight, hairbrush, toothbrush, toothpaste, down jacket, sun hat, long underwear, one extra pair of pants, one extra shirt, underwear, socks, flip-flops, small first aid kit, pocketknife, water bottle, journal and pen, and a collection of small personal items for an altar. I had packed four gallons of water out to my canyon questing site, two at a time, the day before.

The rising sun cast a narrow flamingo-pink strip under a stratum of surging gray clouds. To the north, the fan-shaped alluvium wash disappeared into a V with a fifty-foot sheer rock wall on each side. To the south, great aprons of rocky debris spread out toward the valley floor. Beyond, the cascading ranges of the Panamint Mountains towered in the distance. This was Hanaupah Canyon, the remote, desolate place where I would live for the next four days.

I fished a bottle out of my pack, twisted the lid off, and took a long drink. I'd been instructed to drink one gallon of water every day to flush toxins from my system and stay hydrated—my wilderness quest guide's voice played in my head: *You want C2P—clear and copious pee.* Even in November, daytime temperatures in Death Valley ranged as high as ninety degrees. The water was my lifeline in this desert.

I stood there, surrounded by millions of rocks in all shapes, colors, and sizes—boulders, stones, gravel, and siltstone. I was dwarfed by the immensity of the place. I had brought myself there for a reason. And I was terrified.

At midlife, divorced, my children grown and on their own, I was searching for meaning and a remedy for the unnamable longing that had led me into a series of disappointing relationships. The trauma I had experienced in life—teenage motherhood, marrying abusive men, and serial infidelity—left me with lingering shame and self-doubt. I'd gone to therapy and read a dozen self-improvement books. I'd sat in women's circles, shared my deepest secrets, and listened to others share theirs. Still, something was missing.

More important, I wanted to do something meaningful for my fiftieth birthday. A wilderness quest sounded like exactly the right thing—mysterious and challenging with the promise of spiritual growth and insight.

What healing gifts would nature bring me if I opened myself up to the possibilities?

In the months before the quest, I lost my nerve. I was an experienced camper and backpacker, but the idea of spending four days in isolation without food was unnerving. I had already paid the deposit and told all my friends; I couldn't back out. So I gathered up my courage and showed up. I flew to Las Vegas, rented a four-wheel-drive vehicle, and drove the scenic road west through Red Rock Canyon to Death Valley.

There were two other questers with me on this journey. Karen, a university executive from the East Coast, was questing up the canyon a quarter mile to my right. Debbie, a psychotherapist from Southern California, made her camp three-quarters of a mile down the canyon to my left. Linda and Sara, our guides, held vigil back at base camp, a half mile away on a flat sandy rise.

I wiped drips of water off my chin and caught the faint smell of sage smoke on my hand from the send-off ritual that morning. I remembered Linda and Sara draped in shawls as they fanned sage smoke, prayed over me, and sent me on my way.

"May you get all that you need from your solo time on Mother Earth," Linda whispered into my ear.

"Blessings on your journey," Sara said.

After the send-off and with my heart fluttering in anticipation, I loaded up my backpack and headed west toward my site, or *power place* as the guides had called it.

The memory of the morning sent a surge of loneliness through me. I already missed Linda and Sara and the other questers. I brought my arm to my face, inhaled the musty scent, and looked around at my surroundings. Ton upon ton of rocks spread around me like eons of ancient volcanic memories. I had no tent and no food because exposure and fasting are integral parts of a wilderness quest. It would be the first time I'd attempt to go without eating for longer than five or six hours, let alone four days, and I wondered if I was up to it. I wore an emergency whistle on a lanyard around my neck.

A line from a Mary Oliver poem popped into my head, offering momentary inspiration: *When it's over I want to say all my life I was a bride married to amazement. I was the bridegroom taking the world into my arms.* I had come this far; I would let the Death Valley marriage dance begin, for better or for worse.

I scanned the canyon where I stood, and noticed, for the first time, that my fasting solo site was, regrettably, on a downhill slant. Every traverse across the wash would involve walking cockeyed over the rocky scree. Why hadn't I noticed the slant when I chose this site?

Our two guides had explained to us three questers that choosing our power site, the place we would spend our solo time, was an essential part of the ceremony. We were to spread out and let intuition guide us to a place no farther than a mile from base camp. When we found a place that felt right, we were to approach, ask for permission from the plants and animals to be there, and wait for an answer. The answer might come in the way of a sign from nature or from inside us. The idea of nature as a conscious being with a voice and an opinion was new to me, and I questioned whether it could be true. But the more I thought about it, the more it felt right. It was as if something I had known as a child, but had forgotten as an adult, was coming back around.

On the afternoon the guides sent us in search of our spots, hot and tired, I found this canyon about a half mile from base camp. I chose it because the fan-shaped wash offered early-morning and late-afternoon shade. I didn't remember to ask permission to stay there and didn't notice at that time that the canyon wash was at a gradual downhill angle. I had already messed things up and had only just begun.

Damn it. This wasn't a good site. *I should move*, I thought to myself. No, I couldn't move. My guides had made sure they knew where I was, had even drawn small maps with location X's. I was too embarrassed to consider what would be involved in moving. I perched myself on a rock. Pleading ghrelin growls from my stomach announced the first twelve hours without food. Could I do this? Four days alone in a slanted gravel wash with nothing to eat? No one to talk to?

The guides had instructed us to walk, rest, contemplate, watch what was happening in the natural world around us, create ceremonies, and write in our journals. With only rocks around me, I couldn't imagine anything much to watch in the canyon. On the positive side, even if the time didn't result in any spectacular insights, I might at least lose weight, and walking through the loose pebbles would be good exercise.

A strong wind whipped through the canyon, blew off my sun hat, and carried it to a nearby rock where it pressed flat against the stone. The wind dropped as suddenly as it had begun, leaving an eerie stillness. There didn't appear to be another living thing, only me, the rocks, and the hot wind. I bent to pick up my hat and felt my glasses slip down my sweaty nose. *How long*, I wondered, *before the sun goes down?*

I considered putting my pack on and slipping back into base camp, like an errant pet with its tail between its legs. What the hell was I thinking? There had to be easier and less risky ways to come to terms with who I was at midlife and what I wanted for my future. I could be home sitting in my favorite chair sipping tea. I had never even spent a whole night outdoors by myself, let alone in a place called "Death Valley."

Someone had bailed already. We'd had the initial circle meeting with our guides, and afterward, a fourth quester, an attorney from San Francisco, had driven away without a goodbye. We stood there, looking wide-eyed at one another. One of the guides turned to us and said, "Well, everyone is empowered to do what they need to do to take care of themselves."

The same guide, Sara, told us later that there had been times when people felt complete with their solo time before the four days, and if that happened, we were to come back into base camp. She said once a quester stayed in base camp the whole time, didn't even go out to a solo place. They referred to it as "questing in Grandmother's lap." That sounded much safer, but my instinct told me there was something for me out there in that dry, bleak place that was so unlike my hectic life—commuting an hour to work each day, jamming domestic duties and outdoor fun into the weekend, and starting the whole thing over on Monday morning. My life was so full. The desert was so empty. But even though I knew the quest held the promise of something life changing, I felt like I was subjecting myself to baptism by fire under a burning sun in a godforsaken place.

I put my hat back on and turned to setting up my sleeping area and spirit altar. Three large rocks as big as cars near the canyon wall would supply welcome shade from afternoon sun. I discovered a giant, flat, aqua-colored, waist-high stone that was the perfect place to set up an altar for the things I'd brought from home: a small candle, a round ceramic rattle I'd made for myself, a black-and-gold turkey feather my son had given me, and a leather pouch from a friend. She called it a "spirit pouch." The two-inch square of dark green leather had a drawstring close at the top and held tiny chips of gemstones for support and healing energy: black onyx for patience and determination, rose quartz for emotional healing, and red jasper for strength and honesty. I hoped the little bag of stones around my neck would live up to its promise. And I hoped that I would live up to mine.

I arranged my treasures on the big, smooth, blue-green rock, then stood back and looked at the display. The smallness of the items and the expanse of the stone sent a pang of homesickness through my heart. I looked around at the lonely canyon, the multitude of rocks, and the boundless blue sky. *You'll be okay*, I told myself. *One day at a time.*

I got down on my knees and used the edge of my forearm to level off a gravel area where water had once pooled, pushing the pea-sized stones aside to form a place big enough to accommodate my sleeping bag. The moving gravel pummeled lightly against my arms and made a cascading sound like a wave washing over pebbles on the beach. The noise broke through the hushed canyon, bounced off the rock walls, and rippled back to me. I closed my eyes and pushed my arms through the gravel, enjoying the warm tingle as the tiny remnants of riverbed moved across my skin. I thought about the pouring rain back home in Oregon and the less than two inches of rain that fall in Death Valley each year. It was a miracle anything survived here.

Satisfied that my sleeping mound was level, I walked around the stone-laden ground and picked up four different colored rocks that our questing guides had told us some tribes used to create a Medicine Wheel: red for South, black for West, white for North, and yellow for East. The guides had said that the Medicine Wheel, also called the Sacred Hoop, had been used by Native American tribes for centuries. The wheel embodies the four cardinal directions, called *shields* in the wheel teaching. Each of the shields symbolizes a dimension of health and a cycle of human life: the South stands for the aspect of the child; the West, the adolescent; the North, the adult; and the East, rebirth. The truth of that teaching felt alive somewhere deep inside me.

I noticed that the place I had chosen for my sleeping circle was in the southwest corner of my site. Did the location have subconscious meaning? Should I try to figure out the significance of where I had placed my circle? I ruminated on the meaning of southwest on the wheel for a while but stopped myself from my habit of overanalyzing things and finished making my Medicine Wheel.

At the end of that first day, nauseous and headachy, I turned in before sundown. The guides had taught us a bed-time ritual, and I took it to heart: step inside the Medicine Wheel sleeping circle and pray to the ancestors of the four directions for protection during the night. Not completely convinced it would work, I was willing to try anything to keep scorpions and snakes from creeping into my sleeping bag and lions and tigers and bears from tromping over me. I did exactly what they said. I got ready for bed, stepped inside, closed my eyes, bowed my head, and whispered, "Ancestors of the four directions, please protect my sleeping area from any nighttime dangers. Please keep me safe."

I was unsure of how to appropriately close a prayer to nature. The first thing I thought of from my Catholic upbringing was "Amen." That didn't seem quite right, so I added a simple "Thank you."

Peeling open the sleeping bag, checking for intruders, and finding none, I crawled in and stared up at the purply-blue sky. Again, I heard my guide's voice. *You are a guest in their world. If you stay aware of your surroundings, and move slowly and respectfully, you won't have any problems with animals, insects, and reptiles.*

Lying inside my down sleeping bag was stifling. In Death Valley, the hours warmed until noon, baked after midday, and blazed past sunset. I pulled the covers off and lay exposed in the evening air. Suddenly a surge gripped my gut and my throat watered. Another surge, more intense this time, spasmed through my core. I tried deep breaths to calm the tide but couldn't hold it back. I leaned over and vomited up a bile-stained watery fluid. On my hands and knees, I gagged and choked until my stomach emptied. Retching noises from my vomiting broke through the quiet canyon and created a feedback loop of more gagging and more vomiting. The paroxysms finally ended, leaving me weak and disoriented. I couldn't recall the last time I had vomited. I worried I was getting the stomach flu.

I kept my body flat on my gravelly bed until the sun went down over the canyon wall. A short while later, when the nausea had subsided, I sat up, took in small sips of water, and prayed it would stay down. If I couldn't keep water down, I'd have to return to base camp before my fasting time was completed. That is, if I could walk. As a backup, I did have my emergency whistle (*blow three times, pause, blow three more times*) if I needed help. *So this is what it feels like to starve.* I felt humbled at the thought of all the people in the world who had no food. And here I was with the privilege of not eating by conscious choice.

The light faded to dark, and with it came more hunger and loneliness. It started as a dull ache in my chest, eased up into my throat, and then flooded my eyes. I thought of home, a hot bath, my safe cozy bed with plush pillows, a bedtime snack, a phone call to a friend.

A moaning wind blew over the rocks and shook the brittle branches of the creosote bushes. I watched white pinpoint refracted lights appear in the indigo sky where moments before there had been nothing but a deep blue abyss. I caught a movement at the canyon wall and froze, wide-eyed. A dark blob flitted out from a crevice and flew up quietly through the night sky. Then another and another. I watched, mesmerized, as scallop-winged bats whirled and dove through the air like fluttering whispers. I smiled at the revelation that there were other living beings out there with me in the canyon wash besides rattlesnakes and scorpions. Bats had intrigued me ever since one summer when I was a kid, and a group of rodent-like babies, not yet able to fly, had crawled out from under the siding of our family cabin, and we kids took turns holding the furry, skin-winged little creatures.

Throughout my life, I'd had countless boyfriends and lovers and two husbands and one girlfriend. The partings had left me sad and guilty. As I watched the bats crawl out from their hidey-holes, one after another, I decided this time I wouldn't leave. This time I'd stick it out and prove myself to be a worthy lover—a lover of desert rocks and bats.

I followed the bats' zigzagging dances until it was too dark to see. After dark, I followed their murmurs through the air, first in one ear, then the other. The closer, the better. I fell asleep to the sounds of swooping bats and chirping crickets.

I awoke several times during the night, feeling feverish and threshed by unseen forces, tossing and turning as if in a slow rock tumbler. Each time my eyes popped open, I checked the black void above me to see how far the stars on Orion's sword had moved across the night sky. The constellation reminded me of camping trips with my father.

One of the happy memories I had of my father was when I was nine years old. "That's the constellation of Orion, the hunter." My father pointed to a cluster of stars in the night sky as we sat huddled in blankets around the campfire. "See those stars in a row? That's Orion's sword. You can watch him move through the night sky on his journey." Another memory was crystalized in a photo of five-year-old me cuddled on his lap in my pajamas, a big smile on my face. It was the only picture I had of us together. My father had died from alcoholism when I was sixteen. Family camping trips were my most treasured memories of him.

Now, alone under the stars, I wondered how my life might have been different if my father had been around longer. Would I have grown up more confident? Would I have chosen better partners? I fell asleep missing my dad.

I awoke later lying on my back with the sensation of

something soft and satiny in the hollow of my throat. I gasped but didn't scream. Tiny legs prickled against my skin, and I lay there taking in the odd sensation. Then, calmly and slowly, I scooped up the satiny insect, opened my hand, and released it back into the night air. It wafted away without a sound.

Maybe it was a cecropia moth. Maybe I had been kissed on the throat by a winged messenger from the spirit world. It felt like an initiation, a welcome to my first night alone in the wild, a balm for the inhospitable treatment I'd received weeks earlier on my pre-quest Medicine Walk.

In a phone call with my guides a month before my quest, they had advised me to go on a traditional pre-quest hike called a "Medicine Walk." They said the practice had been adopted from the Native American tradition of taking a contemplative walk in the landscape to ask the natural world for guidance and open the senses to the sights, smells, and sounds of nature around oneself. While on their walk, the quester considers questions like: Where am I going? What must I leave behind? What do I need to learn?

My Medicine Walk had been at Baskett Slough, a National Wildlife Refuge not far from where I lived in Salem, Oregon. I had arrived at dawn, as instructed, with no food, only water, and intended to stay until sundown.

The scalloped edges of rich green oak trees lined the rolling hills of the refuge. Behind the oaks, billowing white clouds stacked shoulder to shoulder, mimicking the arboreal flow of the trees. Stretched out in front of the oaks was a gold-and-brown field of dried Queen Anne's lace. I stopped on the path, breathed deeply, and took in the landscape: honey gold, nutmeg brown, olive green, and dove white, all opening under a mantle of blue.

I spent the morning meandering along paths that wove through the trees and beside ponds alive with geese. I thought about my upcoming quest in Death Valley. How would I fare? How scared would I be sleeping alone in the wild?

The path dipped down a hill and along a dirt utility road. Halfway down the hill, the sound of rubber tires over gravel interrupted the quiet morning. A white pickup with a government insignia on the door rolled up beside me.

The driver appeared to be in his thirties and wore a plaid flannel shirt and a tan baseball-style cap with an embroidered patch that read DEPARTMENT OF THE INTERIOR, US FISH AND WILDLIFE SERVICE. He lowered the window.

"Hello," I said.

"Hi there. The wildlife refuge is closed for bird nesting," he said in an official tone. "You aren't supposed to be here. It'll reopen in April of next year."

"Okay. I won't bother anything," I said. "I'm just walking."

"Sorry. Doesn't matter. You'll have to leave," he said, fixing his eyes on mine.

My heart sank. I didn't belong. I was being thrown out. I turned around and started back to the trailhead. I heard the man's voice in my head: *You'll have to leave*. I had done everything right so far, but I'd been booted out. I knew my emotional response was an overreaction, but being asked to leave my pre-quest Medicine Walk hurt. It felt like a bad omen.

Baskett Slough was the exact opposite of my questing spot. Whereas the wildlife refuge had been abundant with growth and life, Death Valley was stark and arid with most of its life underground. Still, I was learning to love my canyon home. Nothing and no one had given me any sign that I didn't belong. I felt increasingly more welcome. And the kiss on the throat from the flying creature had been like a tap from a fairy's wand, an invitation to open myself up to kinship with those the guides had referred to as *more-than-human beings*.

The next morning, moth dust on my throat, I didn't wash my face, comb my hair, or brush my teeth. For the next couple of days, I skipped all domestic grooming rituals and let myself go natural. I began to feel like another creature inhabiting the rugged space. By the third day, I had memorized the landscape—every giant boulder, creosote bush, spiney cactus, and occasional lizard that covered the rocky terrain in my canyon home. They were all fellow earthlings with whom I shared this place. We were surviving together in the desert.

Loving the place and its beings didn't alleviate the boredom and gnawing irritation of having nothing to do for hours on end. Fasting from food got easier every day; fasting from my to-do list and other life distractions became harder. The hunger had evolved from an ache to a low roar and finally to a hollowed-out emptiness.

I fished a pocketknife from my day pack, cut off a piece of my hair, wrapped it around a small, pink, oval-shaped rock, and placed it on my stone altar—my DNA joined with the other genetic material in the canyon. I drank water and smeared mint-flavored beeswax balm onto my parched lips. I draped my shawl over a smooth, chaise-lounge-shaped rock, took off my clothes, and lay lizard-like across the flat stone. It was something I had always wanted to do, be naked outside with no one around to see my ample hips and breasts. I was a harsh judge of my body. Nudity outdoors felt like a step toward freedom from my inner critic. At first, my instinct was to cover the front of my body with my shawl, but there was no one out here to criticize me, except myself, and I wanted to push that voice away. Eventually I felt more at ease and able to enjoy the warm caress of the breeze on my body. But I couldn't help but look around the empty canyon once in a while to make sure no one was watching.

The rock walls funneled the laser-beam sun onto my bare skin, and I soaked up the rays. When I couldn't take any more heat, I moved to the shade, perched on a cool rock, and scanned the never-ending row after row of purple-gray mountains stacked up in the distance. I extended my arm and measured the number of fist-lengths between the sun and horizon, one for each hour, the way the guides had taught me. Five fist-lengths meant five hours until sunset.

I pulled a three-ring journal and pen from my gear bag and began to write. I described the speckled Easter egg–colored rocks, the lizards that did push-ups in the sun, the happiness and sadness I felt, the solitude, the boredom. The scratching sounds of pen on paper broke through the dense quiet in rhythmic murmurs. My handwriting came out wide and loose and loopy.

After a while, my backside went numb. Tossing aside my journal and pen, I put on my dusty brown hiking boots and my wide-brimmed sun hat, tied a blue hanky around my neck, and walked naked around the narrow canyon. I paced in wide circles under the searing sun. My breasts bounced and swayed, and my safety whistle danced back and forth like a pendulum across my chest. My hips rose and fell in an awkward gait as I trudged through the loose gravel of the slanted terrain. A raven flew over the slot-like canyon, casting a dark shadow over the rocks. *Caaaaaaw—caaaaaw—caaaaw*, as if mocking me: *You're naked—you're naked—you're naked.*

A gray-and-tan-speckled chuckwalla lizard the size of a baby alligator posed on a rocky ledge like a prehistoric statue. The lizard blended into the rocky surroundings so well that, when it moved, it was like a piece of the ground had gotten up and crawled away. The giant lizard spotted me and scampered down over the rocks, up the canyon wall, and into a dark crevice between boulders. I wondered if I was a scary sight to a lizard, tromping around with nothing on but hiking boots, a sun hat, and a hanky around my neck.

Halfway round the circle, I trembled with exhaustion, no calories left to burn. I slogged my way back to a shady spot near the canyon wall, plopped down, and reached for my water bottle. Raising my arm released a fruity, oniony smell from my sweaty armpit. At home I would have rushed to put on deodorant or jump in the shower. But not out here, not today.

One of the guides had said, "When you come back from your threshold time and share your experiences, we'll help you interpret the lessons nature brought you out there." I wondered if I would have any sage wisdom to share when I got back. A wilderness quest was supposed to bring insights and awakenings. Would I go back to base camp with anything significant to say? Was it possible to fail at questing?

I searched the endless blue sky and the myriad rocks for a distraction to fill my attention and stay in the moment. There must be some way to entertain myself. The curving Panamint Mountain landscape stretched out in the distance like a flowing contortion. Drifting and daydreaming and possibly hallucinating, I imagined the humps of the range like the great breasts of a female body, Mother Earth. The foothills wove the curves of her abdomen, the surrounding mountains spread like outstretched thighs. The voluptuous land formed an abundant Rubenesque figure.

Still naked, nothing on but my dusty boots and straw sun hat, I pulled out my sketchbook and began to draw. The landscape scene flowed from my eyes to my hand and out onto the page. I captured the swelling and receding curves—part mountain, part reclining nude—the widespread legs disappearing into the horizon off the sketchbook page on either side. I added contours and shading, looked up at where shadows fell, then back down over my own naked breasts to the page, adding lines—here, where the light fell in repeated patterns, there, where volcanic upheaval left gashes and lumps from birthing new land. I had those same birthing scars on my body. My son was born in 1968 when I was seventeen years old. The experience was chiseled into my memory like a rock petroglyph.

———————————◡———————————

It started with a dull snap somewhere deep and low inside my body. A warm liquid trickled out from between my legs. I gasped, then held my breath. *This is it*, I thought. For several days I'd been having false labor, contractions that would start up and send rock-hard squeezes over my abdominal muscles, then stop after ten minutes or so. At one point we went to the hospital, thinking for sure I was in labor, only to be sent home disappointed.

My husband, Bob, dozed in an armchair across the room. We were staying with my parents at their mountain vacation cabin for the long Thanksgiving weekend. The OB-GYN had said that, since this was my first baby, it was safe to go ahead with the trip, even though the cabin was an hour away from the nearest hospital.

I leaned back on the brown tweed couch and peered over the mounded girth of my midsection. Two continuous columns of puffy flesh that used to be my ankles rose like bread dough above pink slippers. A small foot gouged at my rib, and a bony protrusion traveled across my lower abdomen, lifting the fabric of my blue nightgown like an alien. The baby had been due three days before. I had been calm about giving birth, in denial about the pain of squeezing a small human from my teenage body. But now it was happening. What would it be like? How much would it hurt? Would I scream like women in the movies?

"My water just broke," I said. "I need a towel."

"Really?" Bob asked. "Are you sure?"

I leaned forward, and a surge of liquid streamed down over the couch and dripped onto the floor. Bob froze, wide-eyed. His ears flushed red. His crew-cut hair stood on end as he sat gawking at me.

Bob Howard and I had been married in a quick ceremony in May of that year and were living in Sacramento, California, where he attended college. He was nineteen going on forty, a serious academic student from a well-off Libertarian family. We'd met the summer before while swimming at a lake near my parents' cabin. Bob was bright, attentive, and smitten with me, and by the following winter, at age sixteen, I was pregnant. I dropped out of high school in my sophomore year. The worst part was that all my friends turned their backs on me. One day I was a popular girl on the high school cheerleading team, and the next day I was an untouchable. Everyone was having sex, but pregnancy was considered shameful.

Bob's parents suggested I consider an abortion. But I wanted the baby. In the late sixties, and in my household, wanting the baby meant marrying the father. I convinced myself I loved Bob, that marriage would be fine, easy. What did I know? I was a baby myself, naive and unprepared for marriage and motherhood. I was too young and unaware to pick up on the dominating and controlling behaviors that, in years to come, would lead to emotional and physical mistreatment that bordered on abuse.

My mother entered the living room, saw what had happened, and burst into action. She grabbed a towel from the bathroom and handed it to me. I struggled to my feet, water trickling down my legs. When I stood up, a dark puddle formed beneath my feet on the braided rug, a family heirloom.

"Sorry," I said.

"Don't fret about it," my mother said. "That's the least of our worries right now." She looked at me through her horn-rimmed glasses and nodded her head of curly, dark hair reassuringly. I studied her face, searching for what to do next. My mother had had four children. She knew what was happening and what would happen. I'd read a labor and childbirth pamphlet from the doctor's office, but I didn't remember any of it.

"Let's get you into the bathroom; then you can change your clothes, and we'll go. We have plenty of time," she said. But I thought I caught a flicker of doubt in her eyes.

Bob headed to the bedroom for my overnight bag. I shoved the towel up between my legs and, with my mother's help, waddled first to the bathroom, then into the bedroom. I reached for my clothes. A hard contraction, three times more painful than those I'd experienced in the days before, bore down over my midsection. I leaned on the dresser, wondering how much worse the pain would get.

"Try not to hold your breath," my mother said. "Keep breathing, even though it hurts."

I nodded, eager to follow any advice that might relieve the pain.

The contraction subsided and I struggled into my clothes and lumbered back out to the living room. I put on my jacket, grabbed my purse, toddled to the car, and eased my bulging frame into the front passenger side of my mother's red Ford station wagon. Bob threw my overnight bag into the back next to my mother, then scooted in behind the wheel, and we were off.

White-knuckling the steering wheel, Bob pressed his foot on the accelerator, and the vehicle careened and swayed over the curvy mountain road like a roller coaster. My mother leaned forward and held my hand tightly. Her warm, firm grip was a comfort. I squeezed her fingers and dug my feet into the floorboard. My body had its own agenda, and I had no control, no choice but to go along as my skin and muscles seized, clamped down, and entered the wild threshold of childbirth. I held my breath and squeezed my eyes closed. *And this is only the beginning*, I thought.

"Breathe," my mother said.

Between contractions, I squeezed the fingers of my right hand over my thumb to keep from comforting myself the way that came naturally to me, the way I had my entire life, by sucking my thumb.

Thumb-sucking had been my shameful secret from the time I was old enough to know people wanted me to stop. My parents tried to stop me with applications of nasty-tasting substances and, once, even a thumb guard with sharp metal protrusions that poked into the roof of my mouth. All of it was aimed at breaking my bad habit, but none of it worked. I was a perpetual thumb-sucker, and I liked it that way.

My siblings tried to shame me into quitting too. Once, on a family camping trip when I was eight years old, we hiked a path lined with giant redwood trees. I lagged at the back of the pack in my favorite green-and-white-striped T-shirt. My straight, silky brown hair bounced off my shoulders as I meandered down the trail, swinging a giant scalloped green leaf back and forth with one hand, sucking my thumb with the other. I was in my own distant little world, finding solace in nature. Nature became my go-to place for respite in those days—the creek across from our house, our backyard fishpond, and the dense, leafy redwood forest. I felt protected from ridicule in those places. Nature didn't care if I sucked my thumb.

My older brother disappeared, hid behind a tree, and waited. I plodded along, head swaying right and left with the rhythm of the swishing leaf. When I caught up, he jumped out from the tree and snapped a photo.

"Ha-ha-ha! I have a picture of you sucking your thumb, and I'm going to show all your friends."

His threat didn't stop me. In elementary school, when we put our heads down on our desks for story time, I sneaked my thumb into my mouth. At middle-school slumber parties, I scrunched down in my sleeping bag, pulled the cover up over my head, and faced the wall, hoping no one saw me sucking my thumb.

I discovered sex at age fourteen, but even the thrill and intimacy of sex couldn't replace the solace of my thumb. I thought I'd kept my habit well-hidden. But one night I lied to my parents, said I would be at a girlfriend's house, then stayed overnight with my boyfriend, Max. Max was eighteen, had already graduated from high school, was six feet tall, and drove a fancy lavender cloth-top Chevrolet. I thought he was so cool. The morning after our night together, Max said I'd been sucking my thumb in my sleep. I brushed it aside, blamed it on a weird dream. He looked at me dubiously but let it go. If Bob ever saw me sucking my thumb at night after we were married, he never mentioned it. If he did know, it was most likely the last thing on his mind on the car ride to the hospital that night. But it was the first thing on mine.

After a tense one-hour drive and my pleading with Bob to please stop hitting every bump in the road, we finally arrived at the hospital. By then my labor pains were longer and more intense. I collapsed onto my knees outside the car. Two nurses helped me into a wheelchair and rushed me into a white-walled labor room, cleaned me out with an enema, shaved me, and doused me with an acrid-smelling brown antiseptic.

With my body hairless, scoured, and sanitized, the nurses moved me onto a gurney and rolled me into the delivery room. I stared up at blinding lights and steely surfaces. On a nearby stand, an array of shiny silver instruments lined up on a white cloth: scissors, clips, syringes, needles, and something that looked like giant metal salad tongs. My already speeding pulse galloped faster. I had never been in a hospital before. Everything about the experience was foreign and frightening.

A heavyset nurse in blue scrubs approached the table and placed one hand over my midsection. "I'm going to check your progress," she said. Her demeanor was all business, as if she were checking to see how the Thanksgiving turkey was coming along. She slipped her icy gloved fingers into the most intimate place on my body. I jumped and gasped as she pushed and prodded. I bit my lip and grimaced but kept silent.

"Oh, my goodness," she said. "You're fully dilated." Why was she surprised? Was that a bad thing or a good thing?

"We'll get you ready for Doctor," she said. "But when the next contraction comes, if you feel like pushing, don't push. I want you to pant, like this." She stuck out her tongue and breathed quickly in and out like a dog.

"Okay," I said, eager to comply. But when the next contraction came, the primal urge to push was overwhelming. It was like trying to keep the ocean tide from turning. I closed my eyes, focused hard, and pushed out small gasps of air. Everything in me said, *You need to push this baby out.* The harder the contractions, the faster I panted.

About the time I thought I couldn't hold on any longer, the doctor charged through the double doors of the delivery room.

"How are we doing?" he asked cheerfully.

"Great. She's ready to push . . . more than ready," the nurse said.

Dr. Robinson, balding, wearing wire-rimmed eyeglasses and a wide smile, spread his arms into the blue surgical gown the nurse held out for him, secured a blue cap onto his head, snapped a white glove onto each hand, and took his position at the end of the delivery table. "Baby is crowning," he said. "I can see a patch of black hair. On the next contraction go ahead and push, Glenda."

I pushed, grunted, and pushed more. I held my breath and bore down hard in a tangle of exquisite relief and searing pain. Between pushes the nurse secured a rubber mask to my nose and told me to breathe deeply. While my mind drifted in and out of gas-induced unconsciousness, my body followed biological primal urges and kept to its task.

I came back around to the sound of Dr. Robinson's voice. "Look, look in the mirror," he said. "You can see your baby coming."

Through blurred twilight sleep, I looked up at a small round mirror above me. A bloody, chrysalis-shaped object wrapped in a purply-gray cord emerged from my body, then plopped out into the doctor's waiting hands.

"You have a beautiful baby boy," he said.

The doctor lifted him, and I gazed at my newborn baby for the first time—his wide-open mouth and grimaced face, his head scrunched down into his shoulders, his legs and arms flailing in the air, toes and fingers spread wide searching for something to hold on to. He had a mass of dark wet hair and a bloody smear on his puffy little face. A white cheese-like substance caked in the folds of his neck and arms. He was a gasping, crying baby, not an alien after all.

"He looks perfect," the doctor said. "Got ten fingers and ten toes. Good color."

I collapsed back down onto the delivery table in relief. The doctor clamped and cut the umbilical cord, and the nurse whooshed my baby away for routine newborn testing, treatments, and cleanup.

When it was all over, and I had been stitched up and washed clean, they moved me onto a gurney and wheeled me out of the delivery room and into a hallway where Bob waited. My body trembled uncontrollably under the flannel blanket, the aftershock of giving birth. Bob leaned over me.

"I'm really glad it's a boy," he said.

"Me too," I said. "But a girl would have been okay too. I'm just happy to have a healthy baby."

"Ewww," he said, backing away. "You have really bad breath."

I pursed my lips and held my breath, embarrassed that I smelled bad. When Bob stood back, I exhaled.

My mother came out of the waiting room and into the hallway.

"Congratulations," she said, squeezing my hand. "The doctor said everything went well."

Quivering and teary, I smiled and nodded, then closed my eyes.

"We're going down to the nursery window to see the baby," my mother said. "Then we're going home to get some sleep. You rest up and we'll be back to see you tomorrow."

Bob and my mother left, and an attendant wheeled me down the hall and into a hospital room.

A few hours later, exhausted and exhilarated, I lay in a rough-sheeted hospital bed dozing. A nurse brought my baby wrapped up tight like a little burrito. I unwrapped the blue flannel receiving blanket and peeked at my baby boy's red body, tiny hands and feet, and toes splayed out from the shock of cool air on his skin. He had a helmet of coal-black hair that stood up in all directions on his slightly cone-shaped head. His eyes were small dark slits in his swollen red face. Everything about him said that being born was a rough business.

I rewrapped William James, "Billy," smoothed his hair, and kissed the top of his head. I inhaled his scent, sweet and earthy. He opened his newborn eyes and studied my face. I wondered how much he took in as we locked eyes and gazed at one another for the first time.

I brought my baby to my breast, and when he felt the warmth of my skin on his cheek, he began rooting, turning his head toward my breast, and opening his mouth searching for the nipple. All instincts pointed him toward naked flesh.

As my baby nursed, my uterus clinched and contracted as if a pull cord ran from breast to womb. Primal signals pulsed oxytocin through my body and flooded me with feelings of motherly love like nothing I'd known before. Complete. Fulfilled. As my baby hooked on to me, suckling, I got hooked on the squirming little bundle of new life I held in my arms.

A short while later, the nurse came back in and whooshed my baby away, back to the nursery. I rolled over, faced the wall, and turned to my thumb. My cheeks and tongue formed a suction around the oval shape that fit perfectly to the roof of my mouth, and I fell into welcome sleep.

I leaned back in my camp chair and studied the lines of stretch marks across my own fleshy hips and abdomen. My body had twice ballooned to accommodate the growth of two healthy babies, a son and a daughter. My breasts had blown up to twice their normal size, painful and overflowing with milk. Now, my breasts hung low, like two old ladies in rocking chairs resting after a job well done.

These memories brought forth others. I had thought childbirth had left my body scarred, loose, and ugly. That belief had been bolstered by Bob, who, a few months after Billy was born, asked, "What about those icky red stretch marks? Are those ever going to go away?" After that, I changed my clothes in private, insisted the lights be turned off. I was only seventeen years old, a high school dropout.

Since then, I had been obsessed with losing weight. I yo-yo dieted, lost pounds and gained them back, never keeping the weight off no matter how hard I tried. Through the years I chose clothing that hid my curvy shape and wore underwire bras called "minimizers." I stood sideways in front of mirrors, assessed how far my stomach protruded, wanted it flat, no paunch. I had absorbed the commands from the magazines and advertisements: Flatten your stomach in thirty days. Be skinny like Twiggy. Being too curvy was a character defect, a flaw to be hidden. My self-doubt and self-deprecation took me down a dark hole. In the weeks that followed Billy's birth, I fumbled my way through new motherhood, relying on my natural instincts like a young doe with a fawn. But isolated all day in a small second-floor apartment in Sacramento, hundreds of miles from my family, I felt so alone. Bob was gone all day and late into the evening, busy with college and a part-time job. I was forced to figure things out on my own. When Billy cried, I cuddled him close, and he quieted. I was his entire universe, and he was mine.

I was reluctant to ask for help. My mother was busy with her new empty-nest life, and my older twin sisters, Lea and Dea, had babies at a young age too and were busy with their own families. I desperately wanted to fit into the independent, self-righteous family I had married into. I read the Ayn Rand novels my mother-in-law assigned me, *Atlas Shrugged* and *The Fountainhead*. I had become a member of the Howard clan; I needed to appear superior, capable, well-groomed, and attractive to my husband. But at home in that apartment, alone and isolated, I struggled with doubts about my appearance and mothering abilities. Bob was no help. Taking care of babies was women's work.

Martin Luther King Jr. and Bobby Kennedy had been assassinated earlier that year. While other young people were taking to the streets in protest of oppression, and women were burning their bras, I was trying to squeeze myself into conformity and the limitations of living in a conservative family. I wanted love and acceptance, so I kept trying.

One morning, I stood naked in front of the mirror staring at my sore and swollen breasts and the ripped marks etched across my abdomen and hips. I'd gained sixty-five pounds in the pregnancy. A month later I was still carrying forty-five of it. I would never again look good in a two-piece swimsuit. I would never again wear a plunging neckline or put on a tight skirt and look sexy. I was already fat and scarred and only in my midteens.

My nipples raw and bleeding, I brought my baby to my breast with one hand and squeezed the arm of the rocking chair with the other. I set my jaw and braced myself until the first stabbing pain subsided, and my milk flowed freely. My baby's tiny chin moved up and down as he pulled, stopped, swallowed with a sigh, then continued nursing. I did want my baby to have a healthy start in life but wondered how long I could tolerate the pain of breastfeeding. My baby suckled at my breast, and in a red-hot flush of shame, I sucked my thumb.

After several miserable days, my breasts toughened up, and I began to feel better. Billy gained weight and thrived. I was beginning to think I was a decent mother after all. Then, a couple of weeks later, something happened that pushed me down into an abyss.

It was a Tuesday morning, and I was bathing my baby in the small mint-green bathroom sink. I lowered his pudgy pink body into the warm water, holding his head with one hand, and smoothed a soft soapy washcloth over his arms and legs and under his back and bottom. He made grunting noises, kicked his feet, and moved his little arms up and down. He liked his bath. But then, in one quick movement, it all changed.

Billy kicked his foot out and hit the water faucet. Burning hot water gushed out and splashed over his tummy. He gasped, flailed, and screamed in pain. I jammed the faucet closed, pulled the baby out of the water, and held him close. I rocked and soothed him with a *shoosh-shoosh*, but it must have hurt terribly, and he wailed on. Eventually he calmed down, and his cries turned to fussing, then to rhythmic sips of air as his small lungs worked to replenish oxygen. I pulled him away and checked for burns. No blistering, only a bright red circle over his frog-like belly. He started to cry again. I took him to the bedroom, laid him down on the bed, nursed him, and bawled myself. I sobbed long after he had fallen asleep. I would never forgive myself. I was a terrible mother.

After that incident, I slipped into a dark, frightening place. I had never experienced real depression before. I had read one or two sentences about it in the pamphlet from the obstetrician's office, but no suggestions for how to remedy the "after-the-baby blues" as they called it back then. I knew that my maternal grandmother had suffered from postpartum psychosis after giving birth to my mother, and I feared I might be headed there too. Suicide crossed my mind, but I quickly pushed the thought aside. I would never leave my child motherless.

I tried turning to my thumb for relief, but it wasn't the same. My thumb felt fat and awkward in my mouth, like it had outgrown the space between my cheeks and tongue. I lived under a black cloud for weeks, cried at the slightest provocation—a wrong word from my overworked husband, a song, a commercial on TV. But a spark inside kept me caring for my baby, even though I felt like I was sleepwalking through gray fog. What saved me was a city park three blocks from where we lived.

One bright sunny and cold January day, no longer able to stand the claustrophobic one-bedroom apartment, I bundled myself and Billy up, tucked him into the perambulator-style baby buggy I'd found for next to nothing at a secondhand store, and headed for the park. We turned a corner, and there, in the middle of the cement and asphalt city, was a wide expanse of emerald-green grass, trees, ornamental shrubs, and a sparkling pond. We walked toward the water along a crushed-rock trail that wound past twisted trunks of California buckeye, aromatic sweet bay, and yellow-leaved ginkgo. At the edge of the pond, near a row of cattails, two great blue herons stood sticklike in the water. Mallard ducks waddled around the shore with their iridescent green heads shining like emeralds in the sunlight. I sat down on a bench and peeked into the buggy at my sleeping baby, his pink face surrounded by blue flannel, his thumb in his mouth.

Trips to the park became an afternoon ritual. At naptime I tucked Billy into the buggy and bounced him to sleep along the pathway to the park. I bought day-old loaves of bread and fed the ducks. The mallards would spot us coming and make a quacking beeline for the bench, a gang of wobbling feathered bowling pins. The wildlife at the pond, the fresh air, and the daily exercise were balm for my despair. Life went on living in that riparian landscape, and I began feeling like my life was worth living again too.

At night, I curled into a fetal position with my back to my husband and tried sucking my thumb. But I was the mother now, the one who offered comfort and nurturing, not the baby who suckled. It was time to give up my infant ways. When I felt the urge to suck my thumb, I tucked it under my fingers and directed my attention toward my baby. I took up cross-stitching and made a small pillow for the couch with the words To THINE OWN SELF BE TRUE stitched in gold thread. It was prophetic wisdom that would become my lifelong pursuit.

By my fourth day in the desert, the story I had told myself about my body was changing. I looked down at my belly and

saw something raw and natural. The birth of new land created scars and disfigurement on the Panamint Mountain, left
her body marked and lumpy and beautiful. Childbirth had
left the same traces of upheaval on my own skin. Our amazing bodies had accommodated radical changes from giving
birth. Both of us were givers of life, and our bodies showed
the effects of that tumultuous miracle. We shared bumps,
bunching, and bulges. The female body was never designed
to be smooth, firm, and flawless. It was designed to create
life, host life, and feed life.

I unknotted the hanky from my neck and wiped my
tears. A paper toppled out from the back of my journal, a
page of quotes I'd copied from the vision quest book. I picked
it up and read the words:

> *To this mountain you shall go on a certain night most
> long and dark . . . ask not of any man where the way
> lies: only follow your Guide, who shall offer himself to
> you, and will meet you on the way. . . .*

I read them again and repeated the words out loud: ". . .
ask not of any man . . . follow your guide, who shall offer himself to you." In that moment, I realized that the guides being
offered to me on this journey were all female, round and full
and abundant. Feminine energy was with me on this quest.
My guides, my fellow questers, and my intimate friends back
home who gave me a send-off party were all women. And
it had all started when Lea gave me that vision quest book.

I folded my hands in my lap and savored the surging
landscape that had changed to a soft amethyst shade. The
words *God the Father* came to me, echoed from my Catholic
upbringing. But I didn't feel God the Father out there. I felt
God the Mother. My body was the image of God the Mother.
The epiphany of God as Mother, Gaia, Pachamama, felt truer

than anything the Catholic Church had ever offered. I felt it like a thunderbolt of awareness in my DNA coming back to life. I raised my hands and brought my palms together, then bowed to the majestic mountains. "Mother God has been with me all along," I said. I stayed naked the rest of the day until the sun went down. At day's end, I snuggled down into my sleeping bag and reflected on the teaching I'd received from the Death Valley landscape—the earth reflected in my body; my body reflected in the earth.

On the last morning in Hanaupah Canyon, I woke up to pale light seeping under a low, heavy dawn. Backlit silhouettes of creosote bushes lined the canyon edge, and crickets chirped in the last hours before sunlight. It was the day I would complete my threshold time and head back to base camp. Although I had become comfortable with the isolation and felt I could stay even longer, the thought of food was a powerful incentive, and I couldn't get up and moving fast enough. I pulled on a pair of lightweight pants and a shirt. The early-morning air was mild, hinting at another warm day in the desert. But it didn't matter how hot it got that day because I'd be sitting in the shade at base camp, breaking my fast and visiting with my questing sisters.

I shoved my gear into my backpack, cinched it closed, and fastened the outside straps. I tied the four empty plastic water containers to the pack. Drinking a gallon every day seemed impossible at first, but I had done it, and it had kept me alive.

I braced my feet and pulled up on the pack, but it didn't budge. Weak and exhausted, I sat down on a rock and studied the bundle. With all the energy I had left, I dragged the pack to a nearby rock, then wrestled it up and onto the flat surface. I backed up to the rock, sat down, and fastened the hip and chest straps. I braced my hands against the rock and stood up, teetering at first, then finding my balance.

Pack secured, I made the slow and arduous journey back to base camp over the loose rocky scree of the canyon wash. My head throbbed. Each step felt like my legs were pulling through wet concrete, but I kept moving. The empty water jugs bounced and clattered against my pack with every step. My breasts hung low and free inside my shirt.

The pastel desert rocks, tar-scented creosote bushes, prickly barrel cacti, and crisp blue sky looked different that morning, glowing, more alive. Morning sunlight glimmered yellow along the horizon. I stopped walking for a moment and took it all in. No longer an interloper, I had befriended this harsh landscape. I hadn't flunked wilderness questing after all.

I ascended the final hill and looked across the flat plain at the tents, tarps, and fire ring that made up base camp. A line of steam rose from a pot on the camp stove: breakfast. My two questing guides, Linda and Sara, stood at the stone-bordered threshold circle, waiting. I closed my eyes, bowed my head, and wept.

At the circle, I slipped out of my pack and let it fall to the ground. I stood at the East entrance, then stepped inside and awaited the homecoming ritual. Sage smoke drifted up from an abalone shell in the middle. Linda, wrapped in a magenta shawl, entered the circle, lifted the shell, and fanned a trail of smoke over my body with a feather. She welcomed me back. Sara shook a rattle over me and whispered a homecoming prayer. I breathed in and let the tears flow. Starburst rays of morning sunlight shone over the voluptuous Panamint Mountains.

That night at the celebratory campfire, the five of us sat in a circle and shared our experiences. Linda and Sara had shaken rattles, beaten drums, and prayed for us every morning and every evening while we were out there. One of the questers, Debbie, had seen a scorpion the first day and spent a sleepless night obsessing about what might be in her sleeping bag. The anxiety became a doorway to reflect on how much of her life she spent worrying about things that were out of her control. The other quester, Karen, made small wreaths out of braided grasses—her way of setting an intention to allow more time for creativity in her life. I shared how nature had gifted me with a new acceptance and appreciation for my body and my epiphany about God the Mother. Time alone on the land had brought each of us what we needed.

At the end of the evening the guides taught us a song:

Earth my body,
Water my blood,
Air my breath and
Fire my spirit.

The words of the song felt like a testament to my experience in Death Valley. My body mirrored in the land, the four gallons of water I drank, the wind that blew through the canyon, and the fiery sunlight that beat down on everything for thirteen hours a day—all summed up in four simple lines of a song.

The next day, before I left for home, I hiked back to my power site in Hanaupah Canyon and stood in the fan-shaped alluvium wash under a clear blue dome sky. I bowed my head and thanked Death Valley for the teachings. I opened my water bottle and poured lifegiving moisture onto the cacti and creosote bushes in an offering of gratitude.

The quest would be the first of many, though I had no inkling at the time that more wonders and profound transformations awaited me in the natural world. I only knew that I had achieved something I wasn't sure I could do. I belonged to the land. I belonged to myself.

CLAIMING
THE ARTIST WITHIN

Let the beauty we love be what we do.
—Rumi

It got cold when the sun went down at eight thousand feet in the Inyo National Forest of Central California, even in midsummer. Fifteen women—twelve questers and three guides—bundled up in hats and down jackets formed a tight circle around the fire. Pairs of dirty boots were lined up around the stone rim of the firepit absorbing the heat while we listened to Anne tell the story of the Inyo land and its native inhabitants. The word *Inyo* meant "the dwelling place of the Great Spirit" in the Mono people's language, and the area had been the historic homeland of the Mono tribe, Coso people, Timbisha, Paiute, Shoshone, and Kawaiisu Native Americans for thousands of years before the miners, railroaders, and ranchers took it over. I leaned toward the fire and jabbed a long stick into a bed of hot coals. The flames blazed up, crackled, and released tiny golden sparks that drifted up and disappeared into the night sky.

The first days of preparation in base camp were phase one of the quest ceremony: the severance phase. During the past three days, I had been preparing to leave my old life behind. I shared my intention in the circle council and talked about why I had come: disillusionment with my job and a longing for more purpose in life. I wrote my own obituary as part of the severance ritual.

The next morning, I would leave for my solo time, four days alone in the wild on my second wilderness quest. I would be praying for insight and fasting from food, daily life, structure, and distractions. I was eager to learn what gifts and treasures my time alone might bring.

Earlier that year, I had been promoted to vice president of human resources, a title I'd worked toward for years and one I thought would bring a sense of accomplishment. But all I felt was tired and stressed. What bothered me more than the extra work and boardroom responsibilities was the recent announcement that the company planned to lay off thirty people. It would fall to me to decide who would go.

Eight top managers of the company, five men and three women, sat around an oval walnut conference table in an otherwise empty room. I crossed my arms and tried to keep a poker face as the company president clicked through overhead slides of charts and graphs explaining reasons for the furloughs. His voice droned on in the background while I bit my lip and clicked through an employee roster in my head. Last in, first out. Louis in the call center, single parent, no college degree. Really nice guy. That one would be hard. Louis had practically begged me for the job when he was hired. Sherry, the new administrative assistant, who had brought me flowers on my birthday. The list went on, people I cared about, people who trusted me. So much for eight years of working to hire only the best people. The employees would hate me. Or, at the very least, fear me.

My first quest, five years earlier (which I thought would be my only one), had been life changing. I wanted to quest again, find what was missing, and feel the sense of clarity and belonging I'd experienced in Death Valley.

I was living two identities, three really: seasoned corporate executive who acted professionally and enforced the rules; a wild woman who had trudged into parts unknown and went for days without a shower; and a closet artist who experimented privately with her creative potential. My mother was an accomplished artist with a fine arts degree. I was a self-taught dabbler who felt intimidated by my mother's advanced skill.

I kept my wilderness and artistic lives quiet and held on to them like secret treasures. My coworkers might think I was crazy to go out alone into the wild without food, but I had done it for my own reasons. I wasn't terribly unhappy, but the feeling that there was more to life lingered in the back of my mind, especially when it came to my art.

Why had I waited so long to pursue what really mattered in my life?

My mother had found her raison d'être as a young child and had been an artist her whole life. She told stories of sketching on any scrap of paper she found on the farm where she grew up, from brown paper bags to receipts from the feed store. To escape from her farm chores, she would sneak up to the attic with crackers, pencil, and paper.

In 1970 I graduated from nursing school. My nursing career lasted for thirteen years until I burned out on nursing and took evening college courses in business and communication with the goal of changing my profession. I started my human resources career in 1983, worked my way up the corporate ladder, and made it to the top position of vice president at age fifty-five. But career success turned out to be an empty prize. I didn't feel like I was making myself or the world a better place. I longed for more joy and sense of purpose.

Sitting around the campfire that night in the Inyo wilderness, I was distracted by a canvas bag on the ground next to my camp chair. Inside were fifteen apple-shaped rattles I'd planned to give away to my fellow questers. After I signed up for the quest, I started wondering about the other women who would be with me on the adventure. There had only been three of us on my last quest, but this time there were twelve. The guides had said that ceremonial rattling with prayer and meditation can be a powerful part of the wilderness quest experience. I decided to bring each woman a handmade ceramic rattle as a gesture of support and goodwill.

Making the rattles was easy and fun. I relaxed into a creative flow as I stood at my kitchen counter, rolled out clay, and smoothed it over round molds. At the right time, when the clay was leather hard, I placed a scoop of bean-shaped dried clay bits inside to create the rattle sound. I wet and scored the edges and pressed the two halves together and then punctured a small hole in the side to release trapped air during the firing. I carved a small *GG* into the side, then blew a blessing with my breath into the hole to expand the clay back out to full roundness: *May the woman who receives this rattle find what she needs on her quest.* It was my way of connecting with the group of strangers with whom I would soon share thoughts and feelings not divulged even to my closest friends. While my hands worked the clay, my heart opened to the idea of sharing my art with the world. The thought of letting my artist self be seen brought tears to my eyes.

When the rattles were bone dry, I fired them and added an oxide stain. The images on the finished pieces—trees, birds, butterflies, bears—stood out in an etched design. All the time I was working with the clay and shaping each round, I imagined who might receive the rattle and how she might use it. The guides say that rattling for extended periods can shake loose stuck energy and bring new insights. While I was making the rattles, I envisioned twelve wild-haired women scattered on mountaintops throughout the Inyo dancing freely, arms in the air, shaking their rattles.

But when it came time to hand them out, I shied away, paralyzed with doubt and insecurity. Voices in my head from past creative failures crept in and sabotaged my plan. Were my creations good enough, or would I embarrass myself? I reached my leg around the foot of the chair and slid the bag back with my foot. If I hadn't told Anne, our questing guide, about my plan, I could have put the bag back into my car and no one would have known. I stood up and squeezed out of the circle, then walked around behind Anne's chair, leaned over, and whispered in her ear.

"I think I'll wait and give the rattles away sometime later, not tonight," I said, feeling my gut tighten as the words left my mouth. In my heart I wanted to go through with my plan, but I dreaded the possibility of the awkward looks and stammering for words that happen when people receive gifts they don't like or want.

"Are you sure?" Anne asked. "This is your last chance to do it before their solo time."

"Yes," I said. "I'm sure. Not tonight."

I felt like a self-conscious little kid. Why had I made the rattles? Was I trying to stand out as special? Who did I think I was?

Later that night I stood in front of dancing flames for the fire release ceremony, a traditional part of quest preparation. Folded in my hand was a piece of paper with a list of all the things I wanted to leave behind, all the things that held me back in life.

"This is my prayer," I said to the fire. "I release all the second-guessing, insecurity, self-doubt, and fear that keep me from pursuing my art." I bent down and picked up a pinecone from the stack, wrapped the paper around it, and threw it into the fire.

My dilemma about the rattles was more than a question of courage. The rattle giveaway represented stepping out from my mother's shadow and, with no art degree and no professional training, claiming the title of artist for myself. I wanted to find out what sort of artist I would have been had I not squatted in the shade of my mother's success.

Earlier that day, Anne and I had sat together in the cool shadows of a pinyon pine tree. Its sweeping branches started just high enough up to allow space for us to duck in beneath. The ground below the pine was a soft earthy duff of cast-off twigs and needles.

"This will probably sound strange," I said, brushing hair away from my face, "but the reason I asked to meet with you is because ever since I got here, I've been crying. Over nothing." A breeze whipped through, lifted the branches of the tree, then laid them back down like the stop-and-start motion of my tears.

"I'm not usually this emotional," I said, "but I feel so torn up, and I'm hoping you can help me figure out what's going on?"

Anne sat across from me in a low camp chair. She wore capri pants and a T-shirt with a water scene and the words Save Mono Lake. In her lap was a black spiral-bound notebook and a ballpoint pen. She had soft, kind-looking eyes that wrinkled at the corners, light freckles, and a leafy curl to her short gray-brown hair.

I sat cross-legged in front of her, nervous and worried about the tears, my body tight and tense. I leaned forward as I spoke, hands grasping my ankles.

"It started the day I got here," I said, "when I saw that black rock-lined ridge out beyond base camp. See the one with the huge tree?" I pointed west toward the distant ridge. On top of the level plateau was a lone juniper tree with masses of cloud-shaped dark green foliage.

I pressed my fist in under my nose. "Here I go again," I said. "I'm sorry."

"Your tears are welcome, GG," Anne said. "Let them flow."

Anne's advice to cry freely was all it took for me to break into an audible sob. I leaned over, covered my face with my hands, and let it go. Anne stayed silent and let me cry. When I was all cried out for the moment, I wiped my eyes, blew my nose, and continued.

"I don't get it," I said. "I love being out here, and I don't really have anything to be so sad about. I came on this quest to get more confidence in my art."

"Could you be crying Earth's tears?" Anne asked. "Maybe you're feeling her sorrow?"

My first reaction to the idea that I was crying Earth's tears was skepticism, but I brushed my doubt aside. After all, wasn't I here to explore my connection to nature and uncover deeper truths? And wasn't it possible that I was engaging in a conversation with the earth that was deeper than words?

Anne encouraged me to lie down on the ground, have a conversation with Mother Earth, ask for what I needed, and then be quiet and listen for an answer.

"I was hoping to come out here and have a peaceful experience. I didn't think I'd be lying on the ground crying my eyes out," I said with a somber chuckle.

"You get what comes on a wilderness quest," she said. "We don't always get to choose."

Anne was rooted and calm, like a tree growing out of the earth. She had an aura of wisdom and confidence that I found comforting, so I listened carefully to her every word. She picked up the journal from her lap and tore out a page. Then she drew on the paper and handed it to me. "You are being given the gift of tears, GG. Go out and find out what those tears are about."

I glanced at the picture, then folded the paper and shoved it into my pocket. "Thank you," I said. "I'll try."

Later, back at my base camp tent site, I unfolded my chair and plopped down with a sigh. I looked up at the wispy sweeping white clouds scattered over the cerulean sky—*mare's tail* clouds, the guides called them—and for a moment, I wanted to leap onto my rubber-tired horse and ride away home. But something had brought me to the Inyo, and if my tears were a gateway to finding out what that was, I was willing to stay and see it through to the end, stuffed-up nose, burning eyes, and all.

I pulled Anne's drawing from my pocket; it was a circle with N, S, E, and W marked at the cardinal direction points, a Medicine Wheel. In the middle of the circle, she had drawn a stick figure bowing to a lollipop tree. The simple childlike artwork contrasted with her elder wisdom. I smiled and held it to my heart.

Anne's comment about crying Mother Earth's tears stayed with me. I wasn't sure I believed it, or that I even understood what she meant. The idea that I was feeling the earth's grief seemed far-fetched. But Anne was an ecopsychologist and psychotherapist who'd been leading wilderness quests for twenty-five years. She was genuine, without a big ego or a need to stand out as a guru or as an enlightened teacher. Her humble nature, vast knowledge, and experience gave me reason to trust her. And it was true that my emotions over those days in the Inyo had been overwhelming and felt otherworldly, like I had stepped into a river of sadness and been swept into the flow. The conversation about tears challenged the boundary between what I thought was me and what I thought was outside of me. If Mother Earth was speaking to me, I wanted to learn how to listen.

———

That afternoon, restless and stirred up about art and tears, I wandered back and forth through my campsite kicking a pinecone. Grasshoppers leaped through dry clumps of weeds ahead of where I walked, clicking like rattles. In one of my favorite Mary Oliver poems, "The Summer Day," Mary described watching a grasshopper eat sugar from the palm of her hand, jaws moving side to side. The last line of the poem reads: *Tell me, what is it you plan to do with your one wild and precious life?*

I reached up and pulled a purply-blue juniper berry off a sprawling limb and crushed it between my fingers. I held the sticky sap under my nose and breathed in a full dose of the spicy, camphoric aroma. The heady scent made me think of my beautiful, doe-eyed daughter, Susie. Susie was in her early thirties, a botany major in graduate school, becoming an expert in plants, herbs, and mushrooms. It was Susie who taught me about juniper berry aromatherapy or, as she called it, *Juniperus occidentalis*. It pleased me that my daughter had found her joy in all things botanical, that she knew exactly what she wanted to do with her one wild and precious life. Her love of lichens, flowers, mushrooms, and the multitude of life-forms that sprouted from the earth inspired me to step fully into my heart's desire too.

To the west of where I stood, the black rock ridge was laid out like a painting in the distance. It was time to go for a hike and get a closer look.

I grabbed my day pack and made sure the ten items the guides had recommended we have on our day hikes were there: map, flashlight, sunscreen, first aid kit, knife, matches, emergency blanket, water, snack, and jacket. On a lanyard around my neck and tucked into my shirt was the emergency whistle I wore twenty-four hours a day. I didn't think I'd travel far from base camp, but I wanted to follow the rules and be prepared. I closed the pack, swung it up, slipped my arms through the openings, and pulled the straps tightly around my hips and shoulders.

After two days of sitting around camp, it felt good to move freely. I was an experienced hiker, and heading out with a pack and a clear destination was one of my favorite activities. I hooked my thumbs around the pack shoulder straps and headed west. My boots scrunched across the dusty ground in rhythmic pace as I trekked through the sparse forest of lemony-scented pinyon pines and yellow sagebrush blooms.

I kept my eye on the open, black rock plateau that spread north to south the length of two city blocks with jagged coal-black rocks that bordered the ridge like a flank of carved sentinels. The lone juniper stood strong at the center of the mesa.

Halfway to the ridge, I stopped to sip water and strip off my long-sleeved shirt. At high elevation, the difference between daytime and nighttime temperatures in the Inyo varied up to forty degrees, with lows in the forties at night and highs in the eighties during the day. With less atmosphere to travel through, the sun's rays intensified on the open chaparral, and I was thankful for a sudden gust of wind that whipped through and cooled my face and arms.

As I came closer, the towering ridge above me was higher than it had appeared from base camp. I tightened the hip strap on my pack and climbed over the heat-absorbing stones, grasping rock ledges, finding footholds, and pulling myself up. At the top I stood under a canopy of green juniper foliage and looked east across the plain to the stone-lined ceremonial threshold circle at base camp and the pine tree where Anne and I had sat earlier that day. My eyes watered again. It was all paradoxical—I felt happy and content to be out on the Inyo land, yet my tearful water table had never been so high.

The twisted, wrinkled bark of the gigantic juniper varied in color from cinnamon at the outer edges to dark espresso in the recesses of the crusted husk. Slipping off my pack, I sat down and leaned back against the sweeping entwined trunk. A slight indentation in the bark offered a comfortable, hollowed-out space for my back, and I relaxed into the lap of the crone-like juniper as if settling into an easy chair.

A movement and a humming vibration startled me, and I flinched. A flash of iridescent green and a blur of wings flitted back and forth in front of my face, then buzzed off with a squeezed chirp. The little creature circled around in the air, then darted back toward me. The hover of wings in my face came with another quick, sharp sound as it flew forward and back at eye level. Then the flying jewel floated and dipped along the black rock ridge and out of sight. Seconds later, the hummingbird circled back and fluttered around my head, zipping forward and back three or four times. It was dizzying and mesmerizing.

The hummingbird flew off, and I replayed the scene in my mind, remembering every detail: shiny black eyes, shimmering green back, a fanned-out russet tail. Was it a rufous? Or maybe an Allen? I couldn't recall the difference between the two species. What I did remember was what I'd read about hummingbirds in a book I had on my shelf at home, *Animal-Speak, The Spiritual & Magical Powers of Creatures Great & Small*, by Ted Andrews. The hummingbird is a symbol of opening the heart to joy, a reminder to find joy in what we do and sing it out. That symbolism, along with the way the little bird seemed curious about me, gave me the idea that the spot under the old sprawling juniper was the perfect place for my four-day solo fast.

"You are exquisite," I said. "Thank you."

I pulled myself up off the ground and brushed juniper berries and leaves from my backside. I swung my pack on, adjusted the straps, and took off across the open chaparral back toward base camp, relieved to have found the perfect power place for my solo fast.

The next morning, after the threshold send-off ritual with Anne and the other questers, I once again traversed the flat open terrain—this time with a loaded backpack on my way to spend four days alone on the ridge. To the right, the Eastern Sierras stood in linear stony arcs under a cascade of cottony clouds. Ahead, the micaceous ridge surrounding my power place gleamed like a monument in the morning light. I felt the now familiar sting of tears and the sensation of light wings fluttering inside my chest. I wasn't sure whether the vibration was excitement or fear.

When I arrived at the plateau, I set up my simple camp-site—a tarp tied four feet up between two juniper limbs, a sleeping mattress that converted to a camp chair, a down sleeping bag, my backpack with art supplies and the ten essentials, clothing and gear, and four one-gallon water containers that I'd brought out the day before. I set up my altar on an exposed root at the base of the juniper. This time I brought a smooth, gray, heart-shaped rock I'd found on a hike, the green spirit pouch filled with gemstones that my friend had given me for my first quest, a marble painted to resemble Earth, and a two-inch Hopi painted bowl that I'd purchased from a trading post on my drive to the Inyo. The bowl represented emptiness waiting to be filled. I placed the rock, marble, and bowl at the foot of the tree, then hung the pendant pouch from a small dry branch above.

With camp set up and nothing else to do, I plopped down into my chair and stared out at layers of puffy white clouds, azure sky, jagged mountain ranges, and brushy mounds of juniper and sage. A low moan rolled through my empty stomach, the first roars of the dragons of hunger, loneliness, boredom, and fear—familiar sounds and feelings from my first quest. I had made it through back then; I could make it now.

The next morning, I awoke to find my spirit pouch lying in the dirt under the juniper. At first, I thought it had fallen from the branch. Looking closer, I realized a critter had chewed through the leather strand halfway around where the string had rubbed against the back of my neck.

"You little stinker," I said, thankful that the creature hadn't packed the whole thing off. I tied the two loose ends together and repaired the pendant, with still enough room to loop it over my head but a reminder that I was a guest in the world of wild things. Everything was up for grabs; anything could happen.

I didn't feel great that second day, but I did need to walk to the check-in spot and move the signal rock back down to let my buddy know I was okay. I grabbed my shawl for sun protection, put on my day pack, and headed off down the hill to the stone pile.

We had all been assigned a stone-pile buddy, another quester whose fasting place was the closest to our own. Every day we each moved a rock, either onto or off the stone pile, showing we were safe and well. My stone-pile check-in place was less than a quarter mile away, down off the ridge and over an exposed field.

Halfway there, dizziness rocked me, and my legs turned rubbery. I went down on my hands and knees and lowered my head. If I passed out, would anyone find me before the sun baked the life out of me? I needed to find shade. I stood up slowly, found my balance, walked to a small pine, and crawled in as far as possible under the lowest branches, rocks digging into the skin on my knees. The sharp tips of the needles prickled my scalp and sent a chill through my body. At least my head and shoulders were out of the sun. I took a drink of water, then curled up and spread my shawl over my exposed legs. I laid my head in the dirt, leaned my back against the fence-post-sized tree trunk, and floated in a vague space between alert and semi-conscious. I had a vision that I was dead, my body floating in the distance over Telescope Peak. Small blue birds held silver threads in their beaks as they flew up and down, dipping in and out, weaving a silver webbed shroud around my body like in a Disney movie. My body ascended toward rays of white light beaming down from the heavens. I wasn't afraid. I had lived a full life. I was ready to surrender to the light.

When I came back to Earth, I tasted bitter metal—toxins burning out of my system from the fasting. I propped up on one elbow, brushed the dirt off my face, and took another drink of water. I grasped the emergency whistle that hung on a lanyard around my neck, held it in my hand, and thought of the sequence: blow three times, pause, then blow three times, over and over until help arrived. I didn't blow it because I started to feel better, but I wanted to know it was right there within reach.

After resting under the pine, my vertigo passed enough for me to walk, and my head felt solid on my shoulders. I made my way to the stone pile and moved my rock, took another sip of water, then walked back across the meadow and bear-crawled up the ridge on my hands and feet, struggling, resting, pacing myself. When I made it back to my site, I rolled into my chair, closed my eyes, and took several deep breaths of gratitude. Then I ripped open an electrolyte packet and poured it into my water. I drank up the lemon-lime-flavored liquid and, in a few moments, felt restored.

The incident made me more aware of my physical

vulnerability and the risks of being out alone in the wild. So, on the last day, except for going to the stone pile, I did nothing but sit under the juniper in my low camp chair, writing and drawing pictures in my journal. The wind tugged at the pages. I held them down. The shade traveled around the tree with the sun, and I picked up my chair and followed.

After a time, I stopped drawing and gazed out at the puffy white thunderheads that stacked up behind mountain ranges. I thought of the phrase *starving artist* that's used to describe the financial challenges artists face. I was a starving artist of a different type. My stomach was long since empty, and I was starving, yes, but I was starving for more than food. I was starving for a more fulfilled artistic life. I'd been paralyzed by self-doubt, judgment, and criticism.

I'd been creative since childhood. I had sewn doll clothes, drawn pictures of fancy ladies, and set up terrariums for the snakes and lizards I caught. As a young adult, I designed my own clothes, crafted greeting cards, cross-stitched Christmas ornaments, rearranged the living room furniture, and made new throw pillows for the sofa. I was creative, but never considered myself a real artist.

My mother held the title of *artist* in the family and had taught art for years. It wasn't that she discouraged me from doing art, but she didn't offer much encouragement or tutelage either. She was too busy earning a living and keeping the household together for four kids and an alcoholic husband. My older brother was the one who was believed to have inherited her talent, not me. I used to sit back quietly and watch him draw cartoons, content to admire his skill.

Plus, any hopes I had about becoming an artist were squashed in junior high school by my seventh-grade art teacher, Mr. Swinford. My brother, Mickey, had been in Harry Swinford's art class two years earlier. Mickey and his friends had nicknamed him "Halitosis Harry."

On a small table at the front of the art classroom was a three-part still life: a blue vase, a red apple, and a yellow lemon. Mr. Swinford roamed the classroom, stroking his pointed Lucifer-style beard between his thumb and fingers—a gesture that appeared more staged than contemplative—and stopped at each table to examine our still-life drawings. In the back corner of the room, I sat with three other classmates: wavy-haired Gary Anderson, the most popular boy in our class; Phyllis Mason, the most popular girl, with thick black hair to her waist; and Tommy Jackson, a cute red-headed boy who caused me to blush and go mute whenever he spoke to me. Mr. Swinford walked up behind my chair, his presence like a demonic looming gargoyle. In the silence before he spoke, I looked around the table and compared my drawing to the other students' work. Not too bad, or at least I thought. Mr. Swinford clasped his hands behind his back and bent down over my drawing. I froze and waited for what I'd hoped would be praise. Forty years later, I remembered his exact words.

"Your proportion is all off. You certainly don't have the talent your brother has," he said, loud enough for the whole class to hear.

I nearly swooned from the stench of his breath and the red-hot flash of embarrassment. I wanted to crawl under the table. *Don't cry*, I told myself, but I couldn't hold back. Mr. Swinford either didn't notice or pretended he didn't and walked away. When the bell rang, I bolted out of the classroom.

Swinford all but ignored me for the rest of that academic year, as if I had personally disappointed him. His thoughtlessness helped squelch any dreams I had about being an artist. I put away my art supplies for years afterward.

In my early forties, I mustered up my courage and signed up for a watercolor class my mother was offering. While the other students followed her instruction and blended soft pinks and blues to create delicate petals and leaves, I ended up with a muddy gray-brown mess on the paper.

"Well, that's one of the things that can happen with water-color—the colors can run together if you're not careful," my mother said. "It just takes practice."

I started over three times but fell short. My purple flowers turned gray. My orange blossoms bled to taupe. It was embarrassing, the daughter of the instructor with the worst painting in the class.

Many times, I had torn up my artwork because it wasn't perfect or thrown away sewing projects because I'd made a mistake. As I sat in my camp chair remembering my muddy paintings, my heart ached for the little girl who thought what she created was never good enough, and for the woman who still felt that way.

The art I was creating under the Grandmother Juniper tree, doodling shapes and rambling lines, wasn't *fine art*. I was creating from my imagination, freestyle. Was that not every bit as worthy as a fine-art technical painting? I was creating art for the joy of it, art that sprang up in the moment from somewhere inside me. I held up each picture and considered the shapes and colors, then looked around me at the same qualities in the land, trees, and clouds. My art reflected the way I saw the world, simple and pure, my version of fine art. I felt a pleasant tingling sensation somewhere between my gut and heart. Maybe it was time I appreciated my art for what it meant to me, not for how others might see it.

Out of the corner of my eye, I saw a golden-mantled ground squirrel come bounding over. I looked up at the little creature standing on its hind legs and sniffing the air. It approached closer, its little neck outstretched and whiskers trembling as it surveyed the scene. Then, as if its curiosity had been satisfied, it romped off into the bushes. A hum-mingbird, perhaps the same one I'd seen before, floated over me, then swooped down toward the colored pencils on my lap and perused them for petals. Seconds later, a flock of mountain bluebirds swooped through the sky and chirped lilting musical trills. All of nature around me was offering encouragement: Stop lamenting! Start creating!

"You're right," I said to the wild things. I wiped my tears and dug into my art supply bag for more colored pencils. I set my chair closer to the big juniper, hunkered down, and continued drawing. I drew the bluebirds, the squirrel, the hummingbird, the trees, the rounded black rocks along the ridge that looked like seals on a beach, and puffy white clouds floating through the blue sky. I let my imagination run free and sketched a self-portrait with big blue teardrops falling from the corners of oversized, brown-as-a-coffee-bean eyes. My illustrations were childlike, with simple lines and bold colors.

When I finished, I carefully ripped the pages from the journal and folded the drawings into a small accordion book. Instead of building a Medicine Wheel on the ground as Anne had suggested, I drew a circle on the book cover and marked the four directions: N, S, E, and W. At each compass point I drew a small red heart. And in the middle, I wrote a title: *Childlike Wonder, by GG, Artist and Creator.*

Storm clouds had been building over the ridge all morning, billowy white at midday, gunmetal gray and ominous later in the afternoon. The sky finally let loose and shed drops of rain onto my miniature book cover, bleeding out the red hearts where the water hit. I liked the effect of how Mother Earth's tears turned my art into watercolor, as if she were creating art with me.

The rain picked up. I packed up my art supplies and sought shelter under the tarp. Raindrops hit the nylon surface, *plunk, plunk, plunk,* slowly at first, then quickening to a full shower. The wind picked up and pushed the rain sideways. I scooched down into my sleeping bag and scooted myself farther back against the tree trunk as I watched the rain splatter and dance on the flat rocks. Thunder and lightning put on a zigzagged light show in the distance. I toyed with the urge to get up, take off my clothes, and dance naked in the rain. I had spent hours naked in Death Valley on my first quest, but it had been warm and dry in the canyon; this day was cold and wet. Shedding my clothes and venturing out from the warmth seemed like a ridiculous idea. What would my favorite artists, Georgia O'Keeffe and Frida Kahlo, do? Georgia and Frida didn't seem to give a damn about what other people thought. They inspired free expression in the moment, with or without paint.

I summoned all my courage and peeled down. Skin pale as a ghost, I ducked out from under the tarp and tiptoed across the shale rocks to the edge of the ridge. The cold wet ground sent a rousing shock up through my bare feet. I crossed my arms around my breasts in an automatic gesture of modesty. Then I caught myself, let my arms fall to my sides, and stood alongside the rocks, trees, and flowers, all of us in our bare natural state. Freezing air awakened every cell in my body. Gigantic goosebumps rose over my bare skin. I felt wild and daring. I shook my body, and the thunder shook back at me. I waved my arms overhead, then rocked back and forth, shifting my weight from one foot to the other, partly to dance, partly to warm up. My white fleshy body contrasted with the dark wet rocks like a goddess in a Botticelli painting. I leaped around, flinging my arms up and down like a free bird.

Then I felt a shift like an explosion of delight. I stopped, planted my feet wide on the stony, ice-cold ground, and raised my fists in the air like a champion running across a finish line. I shouted to the rocks and the mountains and anything or anyone within hearing distance, "I am an artist! I am a maker! I am a creator of beauty in this world!" As if in response, a flash of jagged white lightning illuminated the sky like a searchlight, sending a quiver through my naked body. Seconds later a dramatic crack of thunder reverberated, leaving an ozone scent in the air, a sign that the lightning was close.

The wind whipped my hair across my face. I was freezing cold, remembering the pledge we questers had made to one another not to take any unnecessary risks during our solo time. Being naked and exposed on an open plateau during a lightning storm was not the smartest idea. My feet ached, nearly numbed.

Another bolt of lightning cracked over the ridge. A bellowing rumble followed. More flashes of light and another crackling boom sent me dashing for cover under the tarp. In a nanosecond I went from wild, ecstatic dancing bird to cowering, humbled human. Still, I was exhilarated, and I closed my eyes, savoring my moment of declaration. I was not the same person who had sat in base camp four days earlier and hid the bag of rattles behind a chair. Tears filled my eyes. This time, I knew the reason why. I had claimed my title: Artist.

Pulling my camp towel from my pack, I dried my body, slipped on my long underwear, and cuddled down into my safe lair under the juniper limbs. Tingling in the afterglow, I listened to the rain pummel the tarp and giggled out loud. I had done it. I had danced naked in a thunderstorm, and I would never be the same.

The next morning, I eagerly packed up my gear and headed back to base camp as the sun crested the eastern horizon and cast a rosy hue over the chaparral. I was looking forward to seeing the other questers and sharing my story in the circle council. I struggled into my backpack, cinched the belt tight, and started out. Weak from fasting, I climbed slowly and carefully down over the black rocks and off the ridge. I heard a hummingbird squeeze-chirp somewhere nearby.

"Goodbye, my little jeweled friend," I said. "And thank you."

On my last night in the Inyo, the fire crackled and cast an orange glow over the faces of the women around the circle, each of us with a colorful shawl draped around our shoulders, given to us by our guides. We had all completed our solo fast, and celebration was in the air. What had started out as a time of tears and uncertainty had ended up in a joyful reclamation of my artistic self. I wondered how that awakening would show up in my day-to-day life back home.

Anne leaned in toward the fire and started singing. Each time she chanted a line, she raised her eyebrows playfully, her brown eyes sparkling in the firelight.

> *I've got a rattle in my heart.*
> *I've got a rattle in my heart.*
> *I always know which way to go 'cuz I've got a rattle in my heart.*

I had fifteen rattles waiting in my heart, and the song felt like a call to action. This time, I was ready.

I leaned over and whispered in Anne's ear.

"I've decided to give the rattles away tonight," I said. Anne turned her head and smiled reassuringly, then gave a wink and an affirmative nod.

My face flushed as hot as the coals in the fire as I picked up the bulging bag. I started around the circle, reached in, pulled out one of the rattles, and without looking at it, handed it to the first woman.

"This is for you."

Then I sidestepped around the circle, handing a rattle to each woman until there was only one left in the bag, the one that would be mine. The women, who had been reverentially quiet during the ceremonial giveaway, erupted in praise. "These are absolutely beautiful" and "Thank you" and

"Wow, you really made these?" I was beaming. I had chosen the perfect audience for my artistic unveiling. I reached into the bag and pulled out my rattle, tilting it toward the firelight to get a good look. In the center was the image of a hummingbird. I felt my chest vibrate like tiny wings beating against my heart.

We danced around the fire and shook our rattles, as I had imagined we would, weeks earlier, when I created them at my kitchen counter. That night, exhausted, I was in bed at dusk. Through my tent window, the silhouette of the now familiar black rock ridge rose in the distance like an old friend. I curled up, cupped the hummingbird rattle in my hands, and spoke out loud: "Now I know what I plan to do with my one wild and precious life."

The first thing I did when I got back home was to convert my basement into an art studio, with storage shelves, a work counter, and full-spectrum lighting. I painted the floor a soft blue gray, hung my art on the walls, displayed my ceramics on the shelves, and set up a creativity altar with candles, heart-shaped rocks, and feathers. I hung a small glass hummingbird above the altar, to let my muse know she has a standing invitation to visit anytime.

Unearthing the Past

. . . Let this darkness be a bell tower and you the bell. As
you ring, what batters you becomes your strength. . . .
—Rainer Maria Rilke

Everywhere around me lay rocks—igneous, sedimentary, metamorphic—shiny black, gray-blue with striations of quartz, purple, and gold pebbles. Stones that stacked hundreds of layers deeper than what lay on the surface carried memories of having been hurled far from their original source—the traumatic eruption, upheaval, and flooding that shaped it into what it had become, Death Valley. I stood amidst it all with a day pack and a gallon of water, ready to reckon with my own trauma and upheaval from a decision I had made decades earlier: leaving my children with their father to be with another man. It was time to take my broken heart back to the land for forgiveness and healing.

I had flown into Las Vegas again, rented a four-wheel-drive vehicle, and driven west through the Amargosa Valley into the heart of Death Valley. At Furnace Creek, I turned south on Badwater Road, then made the eight-mile trek over the slow, rough, rocky road back into Hanaupah Canyon. I had gone back to the place that had brought me healing. This time, I was on my own for a day-long quest, without a guide. My intention was to make peace with the demons of guilt and betrayal that had haunted me off and on for thirty years. I wanted to heal the underlying trauma of leaving my children and begin to forgive myself for the wound I had inflicted upon my heart and theirs.

Does forgiveness have to take a lifetime, or can it happen in a single moment of grace?

The night before I left Bob in the fall of 1977, we stood face-to-face in the bedroom and exchanged angry words in strained whispers so the children wouldn't hear. I told Bob I was leaving to be with Rich, the man I'd been having an affair with for months. I had been a good mother to Bill, eight years old, and Susie, three, and a dutiful wife on the surface. But I was the type of person who buried my own needs until the seething mass of resentment and longing rumbled in my psyche and blew up like a volcano. Once I reached the boiling point, there was no going back—boom, I was out.

I had tried to leave before, but Bob found me at the hotel where Rich and I were staying and, furious and unyielding, convinced me to come back home and try to work it out. He said the kids needed me. So I went back and tried to make it work, but it was a short-lived effort. Nothing had changed, and I couldn't settle for a dry, humorless life with him anymore. I was twenty-six years old and longed for joy and excitement. Marrying at sixteen, I had missed out on all the normal adventures that most people experience in their late teens and early twenties. While others in my generation were experimenting with drugs and backpacking through Europe, I was changing diapers and packing lunches.

Rich and I had met two years earlier at a redwood sawmill in Northern California where we were both employed. I was married with two young children and worked as a production analyst in the mill. My husband Bob worked in the forestry division of the same company. Rich, witty and fun, was the production manager. He was ten years older, with clear blue eyes, a thick mustache, and a stocky muscular build.

I sat at my desk one afternoon punching the plastic buttons on a ten-key calculator, tallying the previous day's redwood lumber production. Piles of tally tickets were stacked neatly on the desk. A coffee cup, a pad of paper, a stapler, and a tape dispenser lined up beside a boxy black telephone. I had production numbers to crank out and deadlines to meet. Rich walked through the door in a shirt that matched his blue eyes. I sat upright. He was the boss—good-looking, distractingly so, but still the boss. I had no way of knowing that what would happen in the next few moments would change the course of my life.

Rich leaned against the wall, crossed one foot over the other, and folded his arms across his chest. He held a wooden pipe in his hand and wore a gold band on his ring finger. Red mixed in with the brown of his handlebar mustache. His straight white teeth bit down on the tortoiseshell pipe handle. The scent of sweet cherrywood smoke filled the air. He glanced at my face, then moved his gaze down over my body. That day I had worn my favorite outfit, black slacks with a tight-fitting blue, teal, and gold striped sweater and a wide leather belt pulled snug at my waist, accentuating my curvy figure. The attraction between us was electric. We had been flirting shamelessly for weeks with prolonged gazes and suggestive comments. Rich eased the pipe from his mouth and cupped it in his palm.

"Do you want to meet for a drink sometime?" he said.

"Sure," I said. "When?"

It was clear to both of us without saying so that the meeting would be more than a drink. I was married to a man who pointed out my every flaw. Too powerless to leave him and longing to feel loved, I had looked elsewhere for attention. What I didn't get from my husband I found in extramarital affairs. The first one was with my husband's best friend, then with a doctor I worked for (I was a licensed vocational nurse at the time), then a pharmacist at the hospital. I scolded myself after every encounter. Bad wife. Bad mother. But sex outside my marriage made me feel special, important, desirable—all the things I didn't have with Bob. By the time I met Rich, I was beyond the shy uncertainty of first-time infidelity.

"How about Friday night?" he said.

"Okay," I said.

Rich winked and sauntered out. I stared at the empty space where he had been. The lingering aroma of cherry-wood smoke and pheromones in the air made my body tingle.

That Friday night, we met at a secluded parking lot. Rich had brought two glasses and a bottle of Lancers, the most prestigious wine available in grocery stores at the time. He suggested we skip the drink and drive to a nearby town where neither of us knew anyone. I readily agreed, and we spent the evening in a cheap motel room. After that, bolder and more desirous of time alone with Rich, I'd drive up to his horse barn, where we'd lay a blanket down in the straw and entwine ourselves for hours, insatiable. On those nights, the moon shone through the open barn door, the smell of fresh hay permeated the air, and I felt myself transported to a sensuous, intimate world I'd never experienced before.

Bob suspected something was going on and had asked around the company about Rich. The three of us had been the subject of watercooler gossip for weeks. I kept as low a profile as possible, arriving at work exactly on time every day, eating lunch alone in my car, and leaving the building as soon as my shift was over. I couldn't face anyone asking me about Rich. Bob was a well-respected manager, and I was a production clerk. And an adulteress.

I had tried to let the affair go and be happy in my marriage for the sake of my children. But the desire to be loved and feel special was so strong in me that I could no longer live with someone cold and distant. I loved Rich. My love affair with him gave me a taste of what it was like to lighten up, have fun, and feel sexy and desirable. When I told Bob I was leaving, this time for good, he clenched his jaw and his face reddened. Tears pooled in his eyes.

"You're crazy to leave me for him," he said. "People at work have told me he throws temper tantrums; you won't be happy."

There was no turning back.

"I'm leaving everything with you," I said. "The house and all the furniture, the savings account, and the children. All I'm taking are my clothes, my car, and the fifteen hundred dollars in the checking account."

"Good," Bob said. "You don't deserve anything. Go and live with your idiot boyfriend."

Though I knew leaving the kids behind would be excruciatingly painful—for me and for them—I believed I was leaving them at least some semblance of order to help offset the impact of my departure. I didn't know that the separation would leave a canyon-sized cleft in my heart that would be there forever.

I felt a visceral connection to Death Valley, a land that embodied its own history of instability and radical change. A deep lake had covered the entire area ten thousand years before, creating mountain ranges and cutting true river valleys, canyons, and gorges. Down deep, the stony roots of this place still touched the warm heart of the mother. An eternal trust lived in the land—the assurance that what builds up will be broken down, and what breaks down will be built up again.

As I perched on a stone ledge at the edge of the canyon wash, a terrible ache rolled through my chest as I, too, remembered the great eruptions, upheavals, and floods of tears that had shaped me. Every cell in my body held the experiences I had lived, a rich and complicated landscape difficult to navigate. Loneliness, disappointment, guilt, and betrayal—rock walls of failure I climbed, crevasses of abandonment crossed over, slot canyons of divorce squeezed into and back out of. And on and on—the ripping of flesh when the gateway opened and brought forth new life.

On my first quest in Death Valley, I had seen the curves of my body mirrored in the landscape. On my second visit to Hanaupah Canyon, I was again experiencing a reflection of myself in the land. This time, the awareness traveled through the bedrock stratum and down deeper into the hot inner core of my suffering.

For a moment, it seemed Bob had accepted that I was leaving. He sat down on the bed, hands on his knees, and stared at the wall. Then suddenly he shot up and lunged at me. He grabbed my wrists, pushed me down onto the bed, and pressed his body onto me, his eyes riveted on mine in a raging blur. I yanked my head to the side and squeezed my eyes closed.

Although Bob's abuse was mostly verbal, once before, early in our marriage, he had lost his temper and slapped me across the face. He had not touched me in anger since, so his rage that night caught me off guard and terrified me. I raised my head and jutted my chin up toward his arm, ready to sink my teeth into his flesh. But he held his arms, and mine, out beyond reach.

"Let me go," I said. Searing pain burned into my wrists as Bob tightened his grip and pressed my arms into the mattress.

"You're not leaving me," he said, his eyes narrow and smoldering. Droplets of spit splattered onto my face as he spoke. "You're my wife, and you're not leaving."

I tightened my body and clenched my knees together. Bob wedged my legs open with his knee and pushed his weight down against my midsection, sending a stabbing ache through my crotch. I pulled my hips back and pushed my arms against his grip, but I wasn't strong enough to free myself. The zipper on my jeans smashed into my pelvic bone. My heart clamored in my chest and my hands tingled. Tears burned. I squeezed my eyes closed again.

Adrenaline flooded my body, but my voice came out surprisingly calm and rational. "Bob. Stop," I said. "Think about what you're doing. This isn't going to change anything, for God's sake." I stopped struggling and let my body go limp. "Please, just don't."

A play-by-play litany of sexual tragedies rolled through my mind in those seconds: the confusion and searing-hot betrayal I felt when Pamela Knott's older brother molested me on a green velour couch when I was eight; the mortification of sitting in a police station after my high school boyfriend and I got caught having sex in the back seat of his car when I was fourteen; the heartbreaking shame when my friends turned their backs on me after I got pregnant in my high school junior year; and the secret, frantic, serial infidelity during my marriage to Bob. Sex was a confusing paradox of attraction and betrayal.

Bob stopped, dropped his chin to his chest, and released my wrists. He rolled off the bed and hurled a pillow onto the floor. "Don't think for a minute that I'm going to make this easy for you."

I curled into a fetal position and sobbed, my body shaking with relief that he hadn't gone through with the violation.

If I'd had any doubts about leaving Bob, his actions that night sealed the deal. I stood up, pulled my suitcase out of the closet, and began packing in strained silence—clothes, shoes, jackets, and personal belongings.

The next day, I left Bob for good. It rained torrents. I don't remember what words passed between us. What I do remember is the faces of my children, Bill and Susie, standing in the doorway looking confused. Bob stood behind them, a hand on each of their shoulders. I hugged and kissed my children. "I love you guys," I said, my voice cracking as I fought back tears. "I'll pick you up tomorrow and we'll go and do something fun. I'm still your mom, and we will still be together a lot. I just won't be living here anymore."

The children watched every move as I gathered up my bags. They were not crying, and I didn't want them to see my pain. The shattering in my heart was a telltale sign that leaving my children wasn't the right thing. The old cliché that love is blind was true for me that day. Bob was true to his word about not making things easy for me. Every conversation was a struggle; every child pickup and drop-off, a hate-filled encounter. Part of me felt I deserved to suffer his wrath as punishment for leaving.

Rich and I were married soon after our divorces were final. Bob sought custody of the children, and I didn't fight it. Bob was financially stable and a good father. And somewhere in my subconscious I must have known the kids would be better off with him than with Rich as a full-time stepfather.

In the late 1970s, the idea of joint custody wasn't widely known in California, and fathers usually didn't get custody of their children in divorce settlements unless the mother was deemed unfit. Because I gave up custody, my attorney insisted I sign a release of liability saying I wouldn't sue him for malpractice. The divorce settlement gave me the usual visitation rights, every other weekend, and every other holiday.

I took full advantage of every opportunity to see my children, but the hole in my heart eventually turned into a cavern. The decision to leave them with their father was the greatest regret of my life, and I carried deep shame for the choice I'd made to give Bob custody rights. It was acceptable for a man to divorce a woman and leave the children with her, but a woman leaving her children with their father was considered an indecent act. My family shunned me for over a year. The exception was my cousin Lorrie, with whom I'd grown up and who wrote me a long, kind letter of acceptance and support. I held on to that letter, the one connection I had to my family of origin, as I turned toward building a new life with Rich.

I was the third generation of parents who had abandoned their children. My maternal grandmother had been carried off to a mental institution, my father's addiction had driven him to choose the bottle over his family, and I had chosen to leave my children to be with another man.

I later learned that dysfunctional relationship patterns pass from one generation to the next in a subconscious behavior pattern. Once you heal the underlying trauma and learn the life lesson that you are lovable and worthy of being treated with respect and kindness, the pattern can be broken. I vowed to heal my trauma and break the pattern.

———————

Clouds gained ground over the sun and moved heavy and silent overhead, dragging shadows over the myriad stones polished by ancient waterways. No matter where I wandered in the Death Valley canyon, there I was. And there, too, were the memories I had pushed away for so long. I had tried to tuck the pain of divorce and abandonment into a dark cave in the back of my mind as if it had never happened. I had never spoken of Bob's aggression that night, not even to my therapist. But out there in the lap of Mother Earth, I let myself tumble into the strata of hard memories that lay beneath the surface.

The cloudy sky roiled. I cuddled up against a flat-sided boulder and let scenes from the past flash through my consciousness. I reached out and picked up a handful of rounded flat stones, one for each memory I was prepared to face, and built a small rock cairn.

With every rock I added to the top of the cairn, I spoke another story from my past out loud. The stack of small stones stood like steadfast memory keepers, strong and balanced and, I imagined, willing witnesses.

"And you, polished black orb, are for the time I picked up the kids for an outing and was shocked to see bandages over my daughter's ears from cosmetic surgery that, without my knowledge, my ex's mother had convinced him was needed because she felt Susie's ears stuck out too far and kids might make fun of her."

I continued, rock by rock, story by story. Erratic black veins through a stone represented the time the kids told me their stepmother had spanked them with a wooden spoon in a wild rage. They called her *the step-monster*. In my mind, I called her much worse.

I carefully balanced an ice-blue rock bearing a raised white scar for the day I had to leave the theater because I was sobbing so hard during the movie *Kramer vs. Kramer*. There were other rocks for other memories, each one balanced precariously atop those that had come before, stacked ten high at the end. The cairn was a miniature, monolithic monument of my past, now exposed to the light. I cradled my head in my hands and let the waters flow over the landscape of my face, through the tributaries of crow's-feet, and down onto my crisscrossed wrinkled cheeks. What was done was done.

A year before that day in Death Valley, I had flown to the East Coast for a visit with Bill. He and I rode in his pickup along the rolling highway of rural Maryland to see his latest construction project. I glanced over at him. Slight traces of gray sprinkled through his deep brown sideburns. I traced the well-balanced features of his high cheekbones, thick dark eyebrows, and strong, straight Grecian nose. He'd had those big, so-dark-they-looked-black eyes since birth. Bill's eyes were his best feature, both visually and functionally. He spotted wildlife that eluded the rest of us: snakes, birds, wild turkeys, coyotes, deer, elk, foxes, raccoons, and once a rare lynx.

On every visit, I asked to see Bill's latest remodeling effort: a kitchen, screened porch, or room add-on. He did beautiful, meticulous work, and his accomplishments pleased me no end—from detailed cabinetry to fifteen-foot-high decks and pergolas. He had found his talent in life, and his craft was in high demand.

We bounced along the road in the truck while Paul Simon's smooth lyrical voice sang out from the CD player about his wife coming back to tell him she's leaving and his belief that we all would be received out in Graceland. The words of the song conjured up the past and offered an open door of memories that I could either walk through or slam shut. That moment, alone with Bill on a back road, I chose to walk through the door. I clasped my hands together tightly and mentally rehearsed the words I'd thought about so many times before.

"Bill, I want to tell you something that's been on my mind," I said. I took a deep breath and summoned my courage. My son kept his eyes on the road and waited quietly.

"I want to tell you I am sorry for all the pain and difficulty I caused you and your sister when I divorced your dad and left you with him." My breath shortened and the tears burned, but I pushed back the emotion and kept focused on what I wanted to say.

"Well, you are forgiven," Bill said, with a tone of finality, as if to say *and that's that.* I smiled at my son's brevity and confidence.

"Really?" I said. "Just like that?"

"Living with Dad was actually good," Bill said, "until he married Karen. We hated Karen." He let out a short forceful exhale through his nose in what sounded like part laughter, part disgust.

Bob had married Karen two years after the divorce and had two more children, both boys. The way Karen treated Bill, Susie, and me was steeped in resentment. We were Bob's first family and, no doubt, a threat to the security of her own litter of pups.

"I know you did," I said, "and I'm sorry about that too."

"It's not your fault, Mom," Bill said. "You did what you had to do, and it all ended up okay in the end."

Bill's reassurance touched me deeply. I turned my head and watched tear-blurred images of hardwood trees and green meadows flash by the truck window. "I guess we all make mistakes," I said, my voice shaking. "But if I had it to do over again, I sure would have taken you kids with me." I wiped my eyes and looked over for Bill's reaction. He reached out and touched my shoulder.

"Yeah," Bill said, "but that might not have been the right thing either. It's hard to know. Like I said, you did what you thought was the right thing at the time. You can't change the past, Mom."

That's my Bill, I thought. My firstborn child—calm, logical, and encouraging. His words soothed my conscience. His forgiveness meant the world to me. Soon after that visit with my son, I apologized to my daughter too, and afterward, Susie hugged me and said she understood. Despite all the mistakes I'd made along the way, I had raised two intelligent, well-adjusted children who loved me. And if it hadn't been for my relationship with Bob, they would never have been born.

⸻

Overhead in the canyon, things were changing quickly. One minute, clouds ruffled over the sky, and tiers of cumulus decked shoulder to shoulder in every direction, darkening the canyon. The next minute, the wind pushed aside the gray, and rays of sun pierced through and lit up the land. In each moment, the future was being fashioned anew. That was the nature of things in the wild, constantly being altered by wind and weather. But some things never changed, like the earth's resilience and her capacity to rebuild and sustain life. What seemed tragic, like spewing lava and upheavals of land, reshaped the territory into the beauty I saw before me. The same was true for me. Everything that had ever happened to me in my life, all the big and little decisions I'd made along the way, had brought me to that moment in Death Valley when the paradigm through which I had been viewing my past shifted.

I thought of my son's words that day in the truck: *That might not have been the right thing either. It's hard to know . . . you did what you thought was the right thing at the time.* I had deeply appreciated his wisdom at the time, but now I was ready to open myself up and let those words in. If my children were openhearted and loving enough to forgive me, I needed to follow their lead and forgive myself.

I wondered about the possibility that leaving my children with their father when we divorced, and not uprooting them to live with Rich as a full-time stepfather, was the exact right thing to do. The disruption to their lives caused heartache for them and for me, but what if, in the bigger picture, living with their father had been in their highest good and his and mine? I had tried hard through the years to be a good mother: generous, attentive, and understanding, even more so because of what I had done. Would I have been as good a mother if I hadn't worked so hard trying to make up for the past? I had done the best I could with what I knew in the moment. It's possible there are no mistakes in life, only opportunities to learn and grow.

A ray of sun beamed through the canyon and lit up the sinuous formations of the technicolor terrain in a stunning sweep of pink, purple, and blue. I tilted my head back against the rock, squinted into the sky, and let the light of forgiveness stream over my face.

FINDING MY
MEDICINE NAME

What you seek is also seeking you.
—Rumi

Journal and pen in hand, I sat back against a two-hundred-foot-tall Douglas fir tree and waited for inspiration. The Doug fir was the tallest in the area, a mother tree that supported the little trees that grew nearby and supplied them with nutrients through her root system. Around me were waist-high fir trees with tips of feathery new growth that glowed bright green in the sunlight. This was the North Cascades wilderness, a fairyland of mosses, ferns, and lacy-leafed flora in every imaginable shade of green: spring, emerald, seafoam, and pine. I imagined elves, gnomes, and trolls hiding in the greenery, especially after two days of fasting when my senses were on high alert. Plenty of inspiration, but I was distracted by something else.

Twenty feet up the side of a bigleaf maple tree across from where I sat, a heart-shaped hole as wide as the tree trunk itself opened into black space. Gray bark curled in around the edges where the tree had healed over the dinner-plate-sized wound. At the bottom of the heart was a thick line of powdery orange sawdust where sharp claws had carved into the wood. The empty dark space, contrasted with the textured bark, made it look like the tree was solid halfway up, then a blackened patch of nothing, then solid again.

"If you come across a black hole, spend time staring into the abyss and see what's there," Anne once said on a quest years earlier. "You might be surprised by what appears." Staring into dark nothingness. That was contrary to my tendency to think I should be doing something productive. But I was out there, once again, to go against my grain and do things differently, so I was willing to sit and keep an eye on that black hole in the bigleaf maple. I was curious about the hole, too, and any teaching it might have to offer. So far, after two days of watching and waiting, nothing had come to me.

My intention for the Cascadia quest was to consider more closely what it meant to be a loving grandmother. I'd had no role models to emulate. Despite having nine grandchildren of her own, my mother hadn't taken to the role and was not close with her grandchildren. I'd never known any of my grandparents, so I had no firsthand experience.

A week earlier, I'd sat in my daughter's dining room with my grandchildren, Thea and Silas. Paper, scissors, glue, and glitter were scattered on the table in front of us.

"Where are you going, Grandma?" asked seven-year-old Thea, who could have been her brother's twin even though he was three years younger. Both of their faces were fringed with soft brown curls, and both had their mother's doe-brown eyes.

"On a wilderness quest," I said. "It's sort of like camping."

"Are you going to sleep outside?"

"Yes," I said.

"Can we go?" Silas asked.

"Not this time, sweetie," I said. "A wilderness quest is something you do all alone. But I'll take you camping when the weather gets warmer."

"Yay!" he shouted.

The children worked intently collaging tissue paper onto wooden hearts, both with furrowed brows as they concentrated on their creations. They brushed thick gobs of glue and lumpy pieces of red, yellow, blue, and purple tissue in layer upon layer onto the heart shapes, then added garish glitter in mounds over the top. The result didn't look much like the faux stained-glass heart shown in the craft book, but it didn't matter. What mattered was that they had enjoyed the process, each one proudly holding up their artwork while I snapped a photo. "These hearts are absolutely beautiful!" I said. "Your mom is going to love these. We'll give them to her when I get back from my trip." I left them with a promise to return with a new questing story.

———

Staring at a black hole wasn't much of a story, but there it was. And there I was, preoccupied with it. I tried moving on to other things, like drawing and journaling, but the black hole stayed in my awareness, and I glanced up at it from time to time.

On the last day of my solo time, eager for a change in scenery, I grabbed my day pack and went for a hike on a nearby trail along a small creek. The trail wove through a dense forest of lacy-leafed vine maple and towering conifers, their limbs thick with pale green trusses of lichen they call "old man's beard." Every type of fern—sword, licorice, lace, and ladyfinger—dappled the forest floor, relatives of ancient plant species that have lived on this planet for more than three hundred million years. The fern-lined path dipped down and meandered along the trickling brook, then curved back in toward the forest.

In places where the path was overgrown with ferns and salal, I guessed the way, taking care not to get lost in the never-ending sea of green. At a turn in the path stood an empty square of stump bathed in a ray of sunlight. I veered off course and picked my way through the verdant undergrowth for a closer look.

A craggy rim topped the waist-high stump. Not a straight cut from logging, but ragged edged where a windstorm had torn the tree loose from its anchor. Velvety mosses covered the decaying sides of the once-towering conifer. Miniature deer ferns and golden sulfur-capped mushrooms sprouted where the wood met the forest floor. I peered down into the hole, hoping nothing would jump out at me. Long vertical slivers lined with cobwebs formed the inside edges of the hollowed-out stump. Farther down, the roots had deteriorated and disappeared into a deep dark cavern that had once been the heart of the tree.

I took off my pack and held on to the sides of the stump, then lowered my head deeper into the void and caught the musty-earth smell of rotting wood. Two one-inch-long spider egg sacs were woven into a cobwebbed crevice, side by side. Their oval shapes resembled cottony white baby booties, one slightly larger than the other.

The shape of the egg sacs brought a memory. I was eight or nine years old. My mother sat at the dining room table with her head in her hands, crying. A pair of crocheted slippers in variegated blue and green lay on the table. I picked up one of the slippers for a closer look. The stitches were sloppy and uneven, and holes gaped along the top and sides. One was an inch or two longer than the other. Tied at the top of each slipper was a limp tassel that hung to the side like overcooked spaghetti. Inside each was a gray cardboard hand-cut sole with an ink-pen outline showing here and there along the edges where awkward scissor cuts had aimed too far inside or outside the traced line. On the table beside the dilapidated slippers was a sheet of white, blue-lined paper with words that looked more drawn than written. I don't recall the words, only the shaky, misshapen lettering.

"They're from my mother," my mother said, wiping her eyes. "She made them . . . so sad and pathetic."

I patted my mother's shoulder lightly as I studied the slippers and note, then slipped quietly down the hall to my bedroom. Thumb in my mouth, I lay down on my bed and rubbed the satiny blanket edge across my nose and upper lip. It was the first time I had seen any tangible evidence of my grandmother's existence. I envied friends who spent summers with their grandparents in other towns, like the song lyric we sang in second grade: "Over the river and through the woods to grandmother's house we go." I imagined a kind, rosy-cheeked grandmother waiting in a cozy cottage with a crocheted afghan on the couch, doilies on the tables, and an apple pie cooling on the stove.

In my young mind, I thought my mother was ridiculing the handmade slippers, and I felt angry with her. But I realized later that the gift from my grandmother must have incited memories of a lifetime of disappointment, bitterness, and unbearable heartache for my mother.

My grandmother, Ruth Elnora Lehman, was a "manic-depressive," as they called people with her illness back then, who lived most of her adult life in a mental institution. The story I was told was that her illness started after she gave birth to my mother. The baby was taken away soon after she was born because my grandmother had tried to suffocate her with a pillow. Every time Ruth was released from the institution, she got pregnant—supposedly by my grandfather, but no one knows for sure because she became hypersexual in her manic states—and the roller coaster started again: childbirth, illness, institution, five times over until she ended up in the mental hospital for the rest of her life. My mother and her siblings grew up on a meager farm in Iowa, raised by their maternal grandparents, who had already raised six children of their own.

My grandmother's mental illness was an embarrassment to our family, something we didn't talk about. But feeling my mother's sadness and shame about my grandmother's condition, combined with the messages from the Catholic Church proclaiming me a sinner because I ended up pregnant and unmarried at sixteen, plus the family secret of my father's alcoholism, all added up to a young life steeped in guilt and confusion. The underlying message was that there are things that need to be compartmentalized, hidden, and not talked about.

A few yards away from where I stood, the rest of the decaying tree stretched along the forest floor where it had fallen. Several small lime-green fir trees had taken root and sprouted up from the log. It was a nursery tree, a dead conifer that supports new growth from the nutrients of its old rotting wood. The next generation of baby trees was growing along the back of the dead mother tree.

I plopped down on the nursery log, dizzy from the memory of my grandmother's slippers. The thick moss made a soft landing for my backside. I bent forward and, like the memory of my mother at the dining room table, held my head in my hands and cried. I cried for the woman who had been locked in an institution, for the daughter who had lived without a loving mother, and for me, the granddaughter who had grown up without ever knowing her grandmother.

My maternal lineage, the ancient stream of ancestry that ran through me, fell vastly short of storybook perfect. But like the tree under me that had supported growth for the next generation, my matriarchal line had left me a legacy of strength, creativity, and vulnerability. Those women struggled with what life handed them and, in my mother's case, overcame those obstacles to live a full and prosperous life. They had done their best. And I stood on their ancestral shoulders doing my best too.

My mother, GlenDora ("Dodie") Maude Lehman, worked her way through college plucking chickens. She graduated in 1940 with a degree in art and home economics, an uncommon accomplishment for that era. She taught school for twenty-five years and worked hard to support four kids—my brother, two sisters, and me—all while married to an alcoholic. She was resourceful and accomplished. When my mother put her mind to something, she made it happen. She taught me to get things done. She composed over three thousand paintings in her lifetime and sold over two thousand. Being an artist came easily to her. Being a mother seemed more difficult, though. My mother was closed off, emotionally and physically. She was a doer, not a cuddler. Her unspoken motto was: Be strong and endure; if it hurts, push it away. In my childhood memory, she is standing at an easel, painting, or sitting in a chair, grading papers, or reading—preoccupied with something other than her children.

Once, in third grade, I asked her to help me curl my hair the night before picture day, but she had to get student papers corrected and said she was "not good with hair." So I put in the pin curls myself, which was painfully evident in the school photo with my toothy grin and random sprigs of hair poking straight out from my head here and there. It embarrassed me to look at that photo, but it was my mother's favorite of all my school pictures. She had given me a surprising hug and said she'd gotten a kick out of my determination to have curly hair on picture day.

The sky darkened and lowered a curtain over the Cascade Forest, changing the bright green foliage to dull olive. Clouds had been building all afternoon and threatened rain. I high-stepped through the brush back to the trail. Doubling my pace, I managed to reach the shelter of my tarp before the sky opened.

The wind picked up and ruffled through the leaves like a ghostly wraith. I sat in my chair under the Doug fir and reflected on the past days. I had come on the wilderness quest for quiet contemplation and reflection on my grandmother role. My time in the wilderness had brought me three black holes: one high up in a tree, one down in a stump, and the one inside me where I felt the pain my maternal grandmother must have felt about being locked in an institution her whole adult life, as well as my loss at never having known her. My heart ached at the thought of how it would feel not to know my grandchildren, to be isolated from them like my grandmother was from me.

> *How might my new awareness about my maternal lineage help heal past and future generations in my family?*

My eyes drifted back to the hole in the bigleaf maple tree. It took several seconds before I realized the hole was no longer empty. A round curved body, light brown with tan-and-black horizontal markings, became visible in the cavity. It was an owl's face and humped shoulders. The head pivoted back and forth as if on a pendulum. Two large gold eyes circled in black peered down at me.

The owl leaned forward, and its wings opened wide. She

launched from her perch at the edge of the hole and flew over my head. The wings spanned at least three feet, a feathered trajectory gliding through the air above, swift and stealthy like a flying cat. No sound of feathers pierced the air, not one wing flap. Her plumage was tan with dark-lined bars in repeated patterns sweeping across her chest and wings, and below hung sharp talons, an arsenal of knives. She floated into the forest, wove through the spaces between the trees, and disappeared. Owl is said to be a messenger of wisdom and intuition. I wondered what message she had for me.

From the dark forest where the owl had vanished, a blue jay came sailing out, carrying a twig in its beak for nest building, giving me an idea for a ceremony.

Stepping over to where the clearing ended, I scooped up an armload of moss- and lichen-covered branches and fir cones. I spread them on the ground in a sequence of two branches, three fir cones, two more branches, three fir cones, and so on, until they formed a complete circle around me, my own nest. "This will be my quest purpose circle," I said out loud. Purpose circles were another questing ritual I'd learned about from Anne. On the last night of the wilderness quest, the quester builds a circle of good intentions for their life going forward, then stays up all night praying. I stood back and surveyed my work. "This is where I will declare my good intentions," I said.

As dusk closed in, I set up my sleeping bag and pad in the center of my purpose-circle nest and reflected on all my absent grandparents. My father's parents were never mentioned. My maternal grandfather was estranged from our family for reasons I didn't understand as a child. I later learned the sad truth: it was because he didn't care to know us. I never wanted my grandkids to feel that empty black hole. I picked up my journal and wrote: *What does it mean to live my life on purpose? How do I want my grandchildren to remember me?* Scratching sounds from my pen broke through the silence as I wrote across the page: *Encouraging, Fun, Patient,* and the qualities I was proudest of: *Unconditionally Loving and Supportive.*

Unconditionally loving and supportive meant continuing to put my grandchildren first. Yes, I had been a good grandmother. But I had been acting like an extension of their parents at times—disciplining and guiding their behavior. Other times I focused on getting things done and wasn't 100 percent present for them. I wanted to change that. It would be easy to do. I would keep admiring their creations and encouraging their creativity. When they wanted to show me how they'd learned to ride their bikes, I'd stop folding laundry and go outside to watch. I'd listen without interruption to their bathtub stories about swimming dragons and magic mermaids.

Deepening into my role as a grandmother had already started. A few months before the wilderness quest, Bill's daughter, Megan, my oldest granddaughter, had come out from Maryland to visit me when she turned eighteen. Megan and I had not been close, in part because of the physical distance between us but also because my son had divorced Megan's mother when Megan was a toddler, and I had seen her only once a year while she was growing up. Something clicked between Megan and me on that visit. We created art together and talked about her relationship with her fiancé, Jack, who was in the military and stationed in Iraq. We were easy together. Simpatico.

I ripped the pages from my journal and carefully tore around each word: *Encouraging, Fun, Patient, Unconditionally Loving and Supportive.* I added one more: *Nature Teacher.* I walked around the circle and tucked a word under each of the fir cones like a bird weaving her nest. Then I picked up my drum and began beating out a steady rhythm as I walked slowly around the circle. At each of my grand-motherly intention words, I stopped, closed my eyes, and voiced an invocation:

"May I be the fun kind of grandma that my grandkids enjoy being with."

"May I always be unconditionally loving and supportive."

"May I teach my grandkids to love the earth and find joy in nature."

Hearing my words brought me deeper into that recommitment to my grandchildren: grandparenting was a way for me to make up for the times I had missed raising my own kids, times I scolded when I should have listened, times I put my own needs over theirs, all the mistakes I made. Having grandchildren was a chance to do things over and get them right this time.

My days of staying up all night for a purpose-circle ritual were over; a good night's sleep was my priority. So that night, under a blue-white moon haloed in moon dogs—bright refractions of moonlight that surround the orb in ever-widening rings—I turned in early and snuggled down in my purpose-circle nest. The white papers with my grandmotherly aspirations reflected around me like a moonlit wreath of good intentions. I heard an owl call, *Whoo-whoo-whoo—whoo.*

I had heard that wilderness questers are sometimes blessed with a medicine name while on their solo fast. The spirit who gives the blessing can come in any form—frog, snake, raven, coyote, mouse, tree, cactus, or black hole. The name carries with it a mark branded on the soul, and the quester returns to their people and lives out the meaning of their name. When I was in Brownies, the precursor to Girl Scouts, we chose names for ourselves too, like Cedar Tree, Running

Stream, and Acorn Princess. Mine was "Little White Dove," named after a favorite song lyric. Those names were special monikers we called ourselves while we were at day camp stringing acorn necklaces or collecting oak leaves. Walking around my purpose-circle nest that afternoon in the Cascade wilderness, seemingly from out of nowhere, a name came to me: "Earth Warrior Grandma." The little dove had grown into an empowered elder.

Later, when our solo time was over, we questers and base camp guides circled our chairs in a pine duff clearing surrounded by the emerald-green forest. It rained on and off that day, and we dressed in various configurations of rain gear—pants, jackets, and wide-brimmed hats—prepared if the heavens opened up again. When it was my turn to share, I pulled my journal out from a plastic bag and read excerpts of what I had written about the gifts I had received on the quest: the owl, the black holes, and the memory of my grandmother.

"And I have a medicine name," I said. "Earth Warrior Grandma."

BECOMING MY OWN SPIRITUAL AUTHORITY

No one, not even Hafiz, can describe with
words the Great Mystery. No one knows in
which shell the priceless pearl does hide.

—Hafiz

Piled on the living room floor of my inner-city bungalow was everything I'd need for my upcoming quest: sleeping bag and pad, clothes, gear bag, camp food, day pack, water bottles, journal, and pen; plus, things I knew I shouldn't be taking: crossword puzzles, a romance novel, a manicure kit, instant coffee, chocolate bars, cookies, and red wine.

I collapsed in a chair and checked all the gear against the official packing list. It was all there, plus much more. The coffee, chocolate, wine, cookies, and paperbacks were definitely not on the packing list and totally contrary to the traditional practice of fasting from food, distractions, drugs, and alcohol while questing. I was supposed to show up purged and ready for the ceremony.

The plan was to wean myself off coffee, red wine, meat, and high-fat, high-sugar foods at least two weeks before the quest. As the window shortened, I told myself I should get on with it, but I didn't. I didn't stop drinking coffee or wine. And when I thought about starting the purge, my lips tightened, and my jaw thrust up and forward.

I grabbed a canvas bag and started loading the contraband. *To hell with it. I'm taking it all. I might buy some weed and throw that in too.* I tucked the last chocolate bar into the bag and zipped it up, then sank back on the couch cushions, stared at the loot, and shook my head.

An experienced quester, I understood that fasting and solitude were at the heart of the ceremony. On previous quests I'd followed every rule. In my day-to-day life, I paid my bills on time, was a positive role model at work, was kind to people, and kept my toilet clean. I'd raised two great kids, bought my own house, and saved for retirement. Was my feigned obedience catching up with me?

Despite therapy, self-help books, and all my efforts to overcome dysfunctional behaviors, rebellion was creeping back in at age sixty-two. I was railing against wilderness questing, a ceremony I treasured. It made no sense.

I thought I'd left behind the sneaky things I'd done as a kid, like borrowing my sister's doll clothes without asking, plucking the last cookie from the jar, and pilfering the candy bars my father hid in his dresser to soothe his alcohol withdrawal. On Saturday mornings, my mother would drop me off at Saint David's for catechism class, and I'd walk to a friend's house instead. We played Beatles records and danced together on her patio until it was time to meet my mom back at the church. I did this again and again.

During Saturday confession, before Mass on Sunday,

I rehearsed my sins for the priest. I feared my indiscretions were too shameful to confess, so I made up less serious ones.

"Bless me, Father, for I have sinned. I disobeyed my mother one time and I fought with my brother two times." Never mind the shoplifting and lying.

I left the confessional and said the prayers the priest mandated, but I might have cheated on that too. The penance didn't deter me, and I went right back to my sneaky ways.

When I got pregnant at sixteen, I had to grow up fast and tried to put my rebelliousness aside. I married into an ultra-conservative family, got my nursing degree, had another baby five years later, and tried to fit in. My in-laws were intellectuals, conservatives who valued education, power, and, more than anything else, money. I had already joined the family with two strikes against me. I had been raised in a liberal Catholic family, had dropped out of school, and was attending night school to complete my GED. In those days pregnant girls were not allowed to attend regular high school.

I worked hard trying to belong and to be welcomed into the family fold. But hard as I tried, I didn't fit into the Howards' money-driven, holier-than-thou mold. I ended up acting out through marital infidelity.

Sneaking chocolate and wine on a quest was acting out too. But what was I gaining by breaking the rules on a wilderness quest? Who was I cheating?

I looked around the house for something for the traditional altar I would create at my questing site. On a shelf was a collection of items from Mexico: small statues and icons. I picked up a four-inch-long flat, curvy, beaded snake, a native Huichol art piece. I wrapped the snake in tissue and tucked it into my bag. If nothing else, I'd have something meaningful for my questing altar.

Perusing the food and gear piles on the living room rug, I wondered how I would pack it all out to my questing site. More than that, I wondered if my quest might already be working me. Sometimes the wilderness quest begins long before you reach the wilderness.

Two days later, I arrived at Lava Beds National Monument in the middle of a hot afternoon. As I crested the hill and stopped the car, I felt the urge to turn around and head back to the comforts of my home, away from all the rigmarole of the quest, away from my guilty conscience.

Ahead, to the left of the road in a clearing, stood base camp. At one edge of camp was a stone-lined firepit. At the other edge stood the threshold circle lined with melon-sized red-pumice rocks. This was the ceremonial place where, two days later, my guide would pray over me and send me off for my four-day fast in the wilderness. In the middle of the circle stood the threshold staff, a five-foot tree branch wrapped in bands of black, white, yellow, and red yarn and decorated with feathers. On the morning of our send-off, the staff would come out of the ground as a symbolic open doorway to the underworld—the period when I would go out alone to my power site to fast, pray, and die to my old self. On the morning of my return, I would be reborn back through the doorway and welcomed into my new life. *No*, I told myself. *I won't leave.* I had come for something, and I needed to see it through.

I parked my car at a turnout outside base camp and stepped out to a blaze of lava-rock heat. A welcome gust of air cooled my sweaty skin as I unpacked my gear and settled in at my campsite. Being outdoors did feel wonderful.

It was easy choosing my campsite—a shady rise surrounded by evergreen trees, far enough away from base camp to allow privacy, close enough to walk back and forth for council meetings. Closed in and confined, the site was unlike my usual base camp locations. There were no sweeping far-off mountain views or open skies to inspire reflection, only scattered patches of blue visible through thick dark green branches. The trees formed a circle around my camp like a fleet of sentinels, or perhaps more like chaperones on this odd quest.

I set up my modest camp of a tied tarp, a sleeping mat and bag, water jugs, my gear bag, my backpack, and a tote that contained my food and forbidden paraphernalia. I was thankful the tote was solid blue and not transparent plastic.

Finished with camp setup, I gathered my things and headed over to base camp for the opening gathering. I greeted and hugged my fellow questers, then took the last open spot and moved my chair around between protruding rocks until it felt solid. I plopped down, took a deep breath, and looked around at the faces. Cara sat to my left, her dark hair pulled back under a wide-brimmed sun hat and a rose shawl draped loosely around her shoulders. To my right, my friend Holly had taken off her boots and socks. Her bare feet were buried under pine needles and dry duff. Around the circle were six other women dressed in shorts, T-shirts, and sun hats, some holding water bottles, others with journals on their laps, all of us anticipating the opening circle of the quest.

Anne took off her sunglasses and adjusted herself in her chair, then leaned forward and lit the sage for the smudging ritual. A gray plume wafted up from the abalone shell. She waved the smoke around her gray hair and sturdy body, then passed the bowl around the circle. When it came my turn, I held the bowl to my heart and let smoke billow over my face and hair. I closed my eyes. *Let me get my act together and take something meaningful back home with me from my time here.*

"Welcome, everyone," Anne said. Then, ironically, after the introductory comments, she launched into talking about fasting. Anne had never started our pre-quest circle councils this way before. I felt a prickling sensation crawl up my spine.

"I want to begin with a discussion about fasting, the essence of the wilderness quest," she said. "We fast to empty ourselves of food and distractions and let go of any attachments to our day-to-day life. We empty ourselves so that we can be filled with something new."

Not me, I thought to myself. *Not this time.* I squirmed and tucked my sandaled feet under my chair. My red painted toenails suddenly looked ostentatious and out of place. Anne talking about fasting right at the outset was ironic and unsettling. I thought maybe I should gather my contraband, load it in the car, and start over with a clean slate. *Still trying to duck out.* I dug my feet into the earth until my scarlet toenails disappeared under pumice dust.

Anne asked for a show of hands for who intended to fast on the quest. I kept my eyes down and studied a pinecone on the ground. Each outward petallike stipule curved to a graceful point and finished with a sharp thorn at the tip. Like me, it looked good on the outside, but not so innocent when you got up close. I pushed my foot out and rolled the pinecone away. I didn't raise my hand. I wanted to shrink down and disappear.

The other questers all answered affirmatively.

"What about you, GG?" Anne asked. "Will you be fasting on your solo time?"

I had hoped she wouldn't notice, but of course she was keeping track. "Yes, I think so," I lied. My entire body tightened. I knew I wouldn't be fasting. I fully intended to indulge in the debauchery of eating chocolate and drinking coffee and wine during my solo time. I didn't know why, other than that I was dead set on breaking the rules. Now I was in deep. Lying to my questing guide was about as bad as it could get.

Why was I fighting so hard to avoid the lessons that were here for me to learn?

When the day ended, I collapsed onto my sleeping bag under the tarp, but couldn't get to sleep. My deception bothered me. I searched the stars for answers and saw my young self in the confessional at Saint David's. In front of me was the gold glass window covered with tiny holes and the silhouette of the priest's head. On the other side of the partition, he sat in the dark box that separated him from us sinners. I knelt, palms together at my chest. "Bless me, Father, for I have sinned."

I pushed the image away, not wanting to think about my experiences from my Catholic upbringing. Part of me was afraid my mind would go down a rabbit hole and not find its way out; the other part of me felt bored with the old story of the trials and tribulations of being raised Catholic. It was old news, a cliché. I shoved the memory to the back of my mind and eventually found sleep.

The next morning, I awoke to crisp chilly air on my face. I rolled onto my back and caught a flash of a brilliant yellow bird with an orange head and black wings hopping around in the tree above me. I recognized the western tanager. The bird chirped a string of melodic notes as it hopped along the limb. The bright creature looked out of place, as if it belonged in an exotic tropical forest, not in the hot, dry lava terrain. But there it was like a golden beacon of light. I had seen western tanagers before, but never so close. It was a promising omen—another reason to stay.

I stood up, stretched, and dug into my gear bag for a small backpack stove, gas canister, and pan. I set up the stove, heated water, and made myself a cup of instant coffee. Perched on a rock, I sipped the coffee and scanned the ponderosa pines for the tanager, but it had moved on. I hoped it would reappear while I was out there. It seemed so out of place, which is how I felt on my *anti-quest*, as I had named it.

I found my questing spirit pouches and placed the leather lanyards over my head—the green drawstring bag I'd had since my first quest and a new three-inch-square buckskin bag with a small silver feather and a button closure. Inside were gemstone chips, dried sage, and tiny bones. The pouches had become part of my questing ritual. I placed them around my neck at the start of each quest and wore them while I was out in the wild. Each time I returned home, I hung them back on a hook in my bedroom, where they held promise for the next adventure. At least I was continuing one tradition.

I tucked the pouches into the front of my down vest, wrapped a purple ceremonial shawl around my shoulders, then trekked down the hill and through the forest to the pumice rock threshold circle. The circle was the symbolic place where we started and ended our quest solo fasting time, the time when we would go out, supplicate ourselves onto Mother Earth, and ask for her guidance. That was how it was supposed to happen, and that was how it had happened for me on my previous wilderness quests. Time would tell for this one.

I stood at the edge of the rock-lined circle. Eight other questers waited with excitement and reverence. When my time came to step inside and receive my send-off prayers, I stepped forward, my heart pounding against my breastbone, and held my coffee-tainted breath. Anne draped the ceremonial blanket over my shoulders. The weight of the wool felt heavy against my neck and back. If she smelled the coffee, she didn't mention it. I clasped my fingers tightly around the edge of the blanket and pulled it in close to my chest. Anne nodded for me to begin the traditional practice of stating my intention for the quest.

My mind went blank. I had sent the required intention letter to Anne several weeks before, but in that moment, I had no idea what I'd written. *Great Spirit, please send me the words.* I closed my eyes and began speaking.

"My intention for this quest is to connect with something greater than myself . . . to be open to whatever Great Spirit offers me," I said. I hoped I meant it, that I wasn't playing along, being a good girl, saying what was expected to get it over with.

Anne picked up a long black-and-white feather and the smudge bowl, then blew on the burning sage. The embers popped with an orange glow. The earthy smell brought memories of past quests—quiet introspective days, unexpected visitors at night. What would this unconventional quest bring? My guilty conscience turned on itself, and I pictured Anne storming through my campsite, dumping out my wine, breaking up my chocolate bars, tearing up my romance novels. "How dare you lie to me! How dare you violate the sanctity of the wilderness quest!"

Anne fanned the smoke up and down my body and whispered a prayer. "Keep this woman safe. Welcome her into the darkness and bring her the insight and wisdom she needs for renewal."

Amen.

I walked out of the threshold circle and headed west into the forest. The other questers had all followed the normal practice of choosing a different place for their solo time, farther away from their base camp site. But I didn't follow the norm. I stayed put in the original campsite I'd chosen in the dense circle of guardian trees. I felt safe there and didn't want to haul all my gear out to a new location.

The first thing I did when I got back to my site was dig out the chocolate and wine and have myself a rebellion party. I unscrewed the top of a box of wine, peeled the paper and foil from a Dove chocolate bar, and indulged in both. The campsite was my territory to do whatever I wanted. I spent that first day enjoying myself, eating chocolate, drinking wine, and reading pulp fiction.

Again, that night I lay awake under a dark moonless sky. Unsettling questions wormed into my mind. Where had all this rebellion come from? Why had I lied to Anne? Why was I cheating myself out of the traditional questing experience? I clasped my hands behind my head and stared up at stars that flashed in the sky like whitecaps on the ocean. Lying on my back and looking at the stars had become my go-to position on my wilderness quests. It was my pathway into what waited in the dark recesses of my subconscious.

I'd once read that the only way out is through. I knew I needed to stop pushing away painful childhood memories if I wanted to discover the teaching that Mother Earth offered me. I had come on the quest, and I had stayed. I needed to be brave and stop avoiding the unpleasant feelings that accompanied those memories.

It was a Sunday morning in spring 1959. I was excited to receive my first Holy Communion, a religious rite-of-passage sacrament of taking the communion wafer for the first time. I twirled around in my dream dress, white lace with a full skirt, short puffed sleeves, a Peter Pan collar, and three small satin bows spaced evenly down the front bodice. A miniature rhinestone tiara crowned my head, and a shoulder-length lace veil covered my shiny brown hair. The finishing touches were my favorites: soft white cotton gloves, white lace-trimmed socks, and new white Mary Janes. My mother had made my dress and taken me shopping for all the accessories at Montgomery Ward department store.

The group of us gathered like a flock of white lace doves in Saint David's Church foyer and waited under tall and sinewy Sister Carmen's stern eye for the First Communion procession to begin. I stood with my best friend, Nancy, another eight-year-old. Nancy was a dark-eyed, olive-skinned Portuguese girl, an early bloomer a head taller than me. She lived down the street and had an older sister who filled us in on things our parents didn't discuss, like what heavy petting was and how babies were made. Nancy and I exchanged glances and giggled with excitement. Sister Carmen repeatedly told us to quiet down, but I couldn't contain my elation. I provoked Nancy one last time with a sideways peek and a poke with my elbow. We erupted in giggles.

Sister Carmen's bony fingers gripped my shoulders. Her face reddened, and her eyes shot sparks as she squeezed my upper arms. "Stop it, you little pill," she snarled, shaking me forcefully. My head popped back, and my teeth snapped together. "Now get in line!" she yelled.

I stared wide-eyed at the wood floor with tears streaming down my hot cheeks. I wiped my nose with a gloved hand and took my place in the procession line. Sister Carmen turned away, and I stuck my tongue out at her. *You're mean, and I hate you.*

It wasn't the first time one of the sisters had scolded me in front of everyone for talking or fidgeting. More than once, a nun had flicked a finger and thumped me on the side of the head to get my attention. I often had to sit at the back of the catechism class for not behaving.

On the day of First Communion, palms together in prayer pose and perfectly spaced at three feet apart, a line of little First Communion brides step-paused, step-paused our way up the aisle. I held back my tears as we followed Sister Carmen past silky white ribbon bows, flower bouquets, and adoring parents. We reached the front pew, and I scooted in close to Nancy. Her soft arm radiated friendly warmth against mine. I hadn't seen my mother in the crowd, but I was sure she must be there. My father couldn't come to the ceremony because he'd had too much to drink.

The priest started the mass, and Sister Carmen signaled for us to kneel in prayer. The groaning sounds of wood benches sagging and rumbling under body weight echoed through the small church. A pure, white-gloved fist at my chest, I mimicked the black-cloaked nun who had stolen my joy. With resignation in my heart, I recited a prayer that took up residence in my subconscious. I hit my breastbone three times and repeated the phrase: *Mea culpa, mea culpa, mea maxima culpa.* My fault, my fault, my most grievous fault.

I threw off the sleeping bag and anchored my gaze to stars shimmering in the night sky. That prayer of contrition for sinners burned in my gut. Millions of Catholic kids' shining spirits had been dimmed by that prayer—tender, uninitiated kids who were too young to understand the difference between mortal, venial, and original sins. Our family religious practices perpetuated the teaching—not eating meat on Fridays, going to confession and catechism on Saturdays, church on Sundays, and reciting the full rosary at Easter. Then, later in life, I had submitted to overly controlling men who bolstered the lie that I was powerless, guilty, and subservient. *Mea culpa, mea culpa, mea maxima culpa.*

Those messages had woven into my mind like a tapestry of sin, guilt, and shame. It felt like a spool of hot thread was pulling through my heart. I was done with it. I wanted to dig my fingers into the fabric of the tapestry and rip out every strand. I was finished believing that when things went wrong, it was all my fault. Then I thought about all the priests who had sexually abused thousands of children and the Catholic Church's attempts to cover up the crimes, and that infuriated me even more. I smashed my face into my pillow and screamed until my throat hurt. I sat up and spouted a stream of profanities at phantom men in black cassocks. My rage felt exhilarating and scary.

Anger worked around inside my gut that night like a sharp-clawed beast, driving me from my sleeping bag. I had to get up and move to shake off my seething rage. Digging through my gear bag for a flashlight, I came across the tissue-wrapped snake I'd brought for an altar. I unwrapped the snake and set it aside. Tomorrow I would make an altar. For now, I needed to move.

I found my headlamp and pulled it over my head, then slipped on my jacket and shoes and stomped my way down the forested slope toward a clearing. The miner-style beam from my headlamp cast a ghostly blue-white glow over the trees, grasses, and bushes. A tiny moth flickered around the light, its wings banging against my forehead as it tried to land. I swished it away, but it kept coming back, bumping against the light. After several tries, it gave up and flew off.

I paced across the clearing and thought of all the bad choices about men I had made in my life, a series of controlling and emotionally unavailable husbands and boyfriends who, like the Church, had held power over me until I woke up and freed myself. I had settled for whoever wanted me— never thinking about who *I* might want or who was a good partner—and then felt trapped. I had freed myself from my marriages, but getting there hadn't come easy.

In the spring of 1978, I was twenty-seven years old. My second husband, Rich, and I were on a backpacking trip near the Mojave Desert. Beau, our old liver-and-white springer spaniel, partially deaf and blind, trotted back and forth along the trail, running ahead to check things out, then back to us to make sure we were coming. Pine trees and scrub oak grew in pockets over the path and offered shady respites from the scorching desert sun.

We trudged up the steep trail that ascended from the river, narrowed, and traversed a mountainside sprinkled with patches of sprawling manzanita. Suddenly, there was a crash in the leaves up the hill, and a pair of huge ebony-and-rust-colored rattlesnakes, entwined together, came tumbling through the leaves, down the bank, and onto the trail not four feet away from where I stood.

"Shit!" I yelled. Everything happened in slow motion. I stumbled back and bumped into Rich, who was bent over rummaging through his pack. I kept my eye on the snakes and regained my balance.

Mojave rattlesnakes are bulky, heavy-bodied serpents with a breathtaking skin pattern. Vivid yellow color streaks started at the eyes and ran along the side of the head like war paint. There were easily twenty diamonds down the backs of these two, big coal-black rhombuses standing out against butter-colored borders. At the end of each tail was a row of rattles, nine or ten keratinous buttons of clawlike horny material, one for each year of the snake's life.

I watched the snakes pull apart. One slithered down the bank. The other coiled and raised its tail. *Ch-ch-ch-ch-ch-ch-ch-ch.*

Beau, up ahead on the trail, bounded back toward us.

"Beau! Stay!" Rich hollered. But the poor deaf and near-blind dog surged on, full bore, in our direction.

The snake lunged, bit Beau in the neck, and pulled back into its coil. The dog yelped, drew back, and ran up the path.

The rattler slid across the trail and rolled down the hill in a cascade of twisting diamond shapes.

I never saw Rich raise the pistol. The deafening shots shattered my eardrums and sent a rush of fear over me. I cowered down, hands over my ears, eyes watering. "God-damn you, miserable fuck!" Rich shouted. He held the gray steel weapon, a .38 caliber pistol, like an extension of his appendage, his arm popping up with each pull of the trigger. *Pow—pow—pow—pow—pow—pow.* Bursts of dust exploded up from the dry ground where the bullets hit. Then *click—click—click*, the revolver was empty.

"Jesus Christ!" I yelled over the ringing in my ears. "You could have hit me."

Rich didn't answer. Instead, he ran up the trail. "Beau, come," he called.

Rich carried Beau the last two miles of the hike. An emergency trip to the vet revealed that the snake bite had barely snagged the fat waddle on the front of Beau's neck, so the venom hadn't reached his bloodstream.

That was Rich's and my first and last backpacking trip together. It was also the day I admitted to myself that I had married a narcissistic rager.

Over the next years of our marriage, what had once been a fervent entanglement between Rich and me changed. The fire that had burned so hot at the outset of our time together fizzled out. I suggested counseling. Rich would have no part of it. He was not about to "sit in some shrink's office and air our dirty laundry in front of a stranger." He started drinking more. His clear blue eyes that I had found so alluring when we first met turned puffy and bloodshot.

We stayed married, but I began pursuing my own inter-ests. I found my first management job at a medical clinic and attended college at night, working toward my business degree. While I grew more independent and accomplished, Rich grew angrier and more temperamental.

My son, Bill, had come to live with us when he turned fifteen. My first husband, Bob, no longer wanted to deal with his rebellious behaviors of smoking pot and cutting school. My daughter, Susie, who was ten at the time, came to live with us shortly thereafter. Bob had remarried and had two other children, and he was happy to let the kids live with me. And I was happy to have them home.

But Rich didn't like having my children around full-time, and we fought about the kids frequently. It all came to a head one afternoon in 1983. The kids were out of the house, and I confronted Rich about an incident that had occurred earlier that day. He had lashed out at Bill, grabbed him by the shirt, pushed him up against the wall, and threatened to "beat the shit out of him" if he didn't straighten up. That's when a switch flipped in me.

What Rich didn't know was that I had had a pregnancy terminated the day before. I didn't want to bring a child into the conflict and chaos of my failing marriage, and I didn't want a baby with Rich, who acted like a baby himself much of the time. The only thing we'd had in common over those last months of our crumbling relationship was occasional sex. I had been taking birth control pills but had evidently ovulated anyway. It was horrible timing.

Ending the pregnancy felt like the right thing to do, but it had broken my heart and taken me to the edge of my ability to cope. Fed up and furious, I held my ground with Rich, though I stood a safe distance away across the room and glared at him from behind an oak dining table. Threatening to abuse me was one thing; threatening to abuse my children was intolerable. "The next time you lay a hand on my son, I'm calling the police!" I yelled. "You're an asshole!"

Rich stood in the kitchen, leaned forward, and grasped

the edge of the counter as if anchoring his hands to keep control. "You'd better learn when to shut the fuck up," he said, lunging around the counter toward me.

I ducked into the corner of the dining room, ready to bolt, and pulled my arms up over my face. Rich had never hit me, but he'd come close during previous rages. I had backed off and apologized profusely to keep things from escalating to physical violence.

Rich stopped, then squeezed his hands into fists and held them at his chest, one in front of the other in a threatening boxer pose.

I'd had it. It all became clear to me.

When I'd left Bob and granted him custody of my children, it was because I'd wanted to be with Rich so badly that I'd chosen him over my kids. In that moment, I knew I would never again let anyone come between me and my children. Ever. "Go ahead, hit me," I said. "And see what happens." Something in me wanted to bring the whole mess to a climax and get it over with. I didn't think he would hit me, that he was all tantrum and bluster. But after I said it, an icy chill froze over me. The dare might be all it would take for Rich to step over the line.

Rich lowered his arms but kept his fists tightened. "You know," he said in a calculated tone, "I have a room full of guns in there. I could just shoot your ass and shut you up for good." Then he pumped up his chest, turned around, and stomped out of the kitchen toward the den where he kept his guns.

I ran upstairs and locked the bedroom door, jumped onto the bed, curled up, and buried my face in the pillow. *Should I call 911?* If the police came, it would cause a scene; all the neighbors would come out. The kids were due home any moment and would be terrified. But the consequences of not calling could be worse. They might come home and find their mother dead.

I picked up the receiver and dialed the first two numbers, nine, one. The front door slammed, and I hung up the phone. I rolled off the bed, leaped over to the upstairs window, and watched Rich drive away, tires squealing as the truck fishtailed down the road. I slid down to the floor and scream-cried. My marriage was over.

Over the next several weeks, I worried that Rich would come back and threaten me, but I didn't see or hear from him. A mutual friend told me he'd found a girlfriend soon after we separated.

Six months later, I sat in the waiting room of a therapist's office. The brass plate on the office door read BONNIE FULLER, MSW, LCSW. I scooted all the way back on the couch. *Does she know I'm here? Should I knock on the door?* I unbuttoned my blazer jacket and pulled my skirt down over my thighs, then fluffed up the sides and back of my permed hair and straightened my earrings. How could I tell Bonnie why I was there without sounding too messed up? Was I desperate enough to need a therapist?

The office door opened. A short woman with close-cropped, sable-colored hair and an affable smile stepped through the doorway and reached out her hand.

"Hi, I'm Bonnie," she said. "You must be Glenda."

"Hi, nice to meet you," I said, shaking her hand. Her grasp was firm and warm. The knot in my stomach loosened as I followed her into the office.

In the middle of Bonnie's office were two blue, upholstered wingback chairs side by side, a blue flowered love seat, and two small end tables. Bonnie motioned to the love seat, and I sat down, folded my hands in my lap, and crossed my legs. *Here we go.*

"What brings you here today, Glenda?" Bonnie asked.

I tried to answer, but the words snagged in my throat. I curled over, closed my eyes, and pressed my hands to my face. I cried that way, elbows digging into my hips, and rode the tsunami. Then I told Bonnie the truth: that I was thirty-five years old, divorced twice, and single parenting; that I didn't know what I was doing wrong; that my kids were acting out; that I felt like a failure; that I'd been waking up at three in the morning breathless, heart racing, stomach churning, running to the bathroom at all hours of the day and night.

Bonnie reassured me that coming in for counseling was the right thing to do. She said I was suffering from anxiety.

"What is it you are hoping to get from our time together?" she asked.

"I want to be happy," I said. "I want to get over my marriages, be a good mom, and get on with my life. I've fallen into relationships with men who wanted me, and I've never really chosen who I wanted. I don't want to make the same mistakes, hooking up with men who aren't good partners. I'd like to have a happy relationship someday."

At the time I thought that happy relationship would be with a man. I didn't realize that what I was looking for was a healthy, loving relationship with myself. At the end of the hour, my eyes naked and puffy, I uncrossed my legs, relaxed my shoulders, and even chuckled at a couple of things Bonnie said. I had found someone who would help me. Things could be different in the future.

I saw Bonnie every two weeks for nine months. I talked. I cried. I learned from her that growing up in a family with alcoholism can cause certain predictable behaviors, like don't trust, don't feel, and don't talk. But there were two things I learned that resonated the most: adults who grow up in alcoholic households are taught to bury their own needs to please their parents, and teenage girls who grow up in alcoholic households often become more sexually promiscuous to find relief from depression, emotional numbness, and self-loathing. Both described me.

Since my early teen years, I had used casual sex to feel special and wanted. I'd married two emotionally unavailable, abusive men, letting their need for control come before my need for a healthy loving partner. I had rebelled against them by sneaking around with other men, but I wasn't willing to settle for that life any longer. I wanted to find healthier ways to fill the empty places inside me. Bonnie helped me understand that good parenting starts with working through my own dysfunctional habits and patterns. Over the months I counseled with her, my focus shifted away from dating and trying to find the right partner and toward working on making better choices for myself and my children.

On a crisp sunny autumn afternoon, before my last counseling appointment with Bonnie, I wandered in a city park kicking through crunchy dry red and gold leaves. It was my therapy homework assignment, walking alone in nature and writing down whatever thoughts and feelings came up.

Bonnie helped me return to nature as part of my therapy long before I started wilderness questing. I'd spent hours wandering and exploring outdoors as a kid and had forgotten how good it felt to be in the company of water, air, sun, and earth—places in nature that offered reassurance that life goes on. Bonnie was another female guide in my life who had led me back to the earth for healing and solace, a mother figure leading me back to the ultimate Mother. What I learned sitting in her office, along with her encouragement to go out into nature for healing, helped free me from dysfunctional patterns and brought me closer to understanding who I was and how I wanted to live: free from being controlled, free from prioritizing a man's needs over my own.

That night, alone in the dark forest on my wilderness quest, I wanted to free myself like I had before. I was furious at the patriarchal, pedophiliac institution that had planted guilt-ridden and subservient behavior in me. And I knew the only person I was hurting with my anger was myself.

I took in a deep breath and brought my attention to the illuminated ground before me. Earth had offered me pathways to healing. I trusted that she would show me the way. With solid ground beneath my feet, I began walking, weight on one heel, rolling onto the foot, then off bended toes. I repeated the steps, mindfully and slowly. When my mind wandered, I brought my attention back to the feeling of support under my feet, as if I were training a puppy. *Sit. Stay. Come back to the present moment. Come back to the anger—feel the grinding surge of energy. Don't push it away. Stay with it.*

After walking back and forth across the clearing over and over and letting myself feel my anger, it softened. Focusing on the ground beneath my feet took me out of the past, calmed me, and brought me back to Earth. My attention changed to the simple act of walking freely, alone at night in a quiet forest. I returned to my camp and wrote the experience in my journal, then snuggled down and slept soundly for the rest of the night.

The next morning, wind gusts whipped through the trees, littering the ground with moss, twigs, and pinecones. I sheltered against a tree trunk, my legs stretched out and crossed at the ankles. I brushed pine needles from my lap, peeled the silver foil wrapper from a chocolate bar, poured red wine into my cup, then took a bite of the candy bar. The melting chocolate oozed smooth and sweet in my mouth. I closed my eyes and savored the richness. I took a sip of the wine, and the pungent liquid slid over the thick chocolate on my tongue. I held the wine in my mouth for a few seconds, then swallowed. Was I questing? Or was I just camping and calling it a quest?

I leaned back on the tree and leisurely finished off my chocolate and wine. The tops of the tall conifers swayed back and forth in the tempestuous wind. The unsettling flurry stirred everything up, including my candy bar wrappers, which tumbled across the ground. I leaped up to retrieve the papers as they bounced across the forest duff just ahead of my every step, as if someone were pulling them along by a string. Each time I reached out to grab the debris, it blew farther away until finally, I leaped out and snatched it up.

Leaning back against the tree, I suddenly felt a popping sensation high in my nose. A warm drizzle seeped down over my lips and onto my shirt. In seconds, the drizzle turned to a stream. Crimson dots hit the cotton fabric and bloomed out in bright red stains. I grabbed a hanky from my pants pocket and rushed it to my face.

My nose bled and bled, filling the lavender hanky with crimson streaks and clots. I sat still with the hanky stuffed tightly up my nose. Every few minutes I pulled the cloth out and checked for bleeding. When the trickle started up, I stuffed it back in. After a time, I counted to one hundred, then pulled out the soiled hanky. Still bleeding. Another one hundred. Still bleeding. A third one hundred and the bleeding stopped.

When I was sure my nosebleed had stopped, I filled a pan with water, dipped the hanky in, and wiped my nose and upper lip. I dropped the stained handkerchief into the water and watched sanguine clots float to the surface and dissolve into a rusty swill that gave off a ferrous, metallic odor.

At first, I rubbed at the hanky to clean it, but then I stopped myself and thought about what I was doing. I rarely got nosebleeds; a nosebleed on a quest was significant. So

I stopped scrubbing and left the hanky stained with blood. I hung it on a tree limb, and the red-stained handkerchief flapped in the wind like a one-note prayer flag. Barefooted, I stood up and carried the pan of bloody water over to the edge of my campsite. With the reverence of a pagan priestess, I step-paused, step-paused in a slow circle around the grove of ponderosa pines in my campsite, purposely dripping droplets of bloody water as I walked. The thirsty forest duff soaked up the iron-filled liquid like a dry sponge. I imagined nutrients from my blood seeping deep in the ground, down into the lifegiving mycelium that runs like a web of veins under the forest duff.

"May this blood offering bring nourishment to the roots of this tree," I whispered. "And may the root of anger from my Catholic upbringing be absolved."

When the pan was empty, I raised it up and studied the red smears that pooled in the bottom, residuals left behind from my sacrament. I wondered if there was some residual left behind from my Catholic childhood that was also worth salvaging.

At my childhood church, Saint David's, there were two stunning, life-sized statues of Jesus and Mary, one on either side of the altar. Those statues illuminated that otherwise drab church like bilateral holy beacons. While the priest droned on in Latin, I knelt in the front pew with my hands together in prayer and studied the statue of Jesus and the bloody wounds on his feet and palms. At his chest was a deep red heart with swirling orange and yellow flames. Wavy sable-brown hair framed his face and cascaded over his shoulders. Circling his head was a golden halo. I thought the statue of Jesus was beautiful.

On other Sundays, when our family sat on the opposite side of the church, I beheld the statue of Mary shrouded in a cornflower-blue robe. Her head tilted to one side; her hands crossed over her heart. And the best part, beneath her delicate bare toes was a twisted, smooth, sleek serpent with a sagging forked tongue hanging from its mouth. I scanned the undulating beast that wove in and around Mary's feet and ankles and wondered how a snake's body stayed rounded and plump with a person standing on it. I loved studying that statue of Mary.

Those lifelike figures saved me from the long, boring masses I endured as a child. I was delighted when we walked into the church on Sundays, and the first pew was empty. That meant I could sit close to the statues and look for things about them I hadn't noticed before. I never got tired of staring at those figures. They were my earliest memories of appreciating works of art.

I placed the empty pan under the big ponderosa next to the beaded snake. The stained hanky fluttered in the air overhead. It was a holy trinity altar shrine—the bloodstained handkerchief, the Huichol snake, and the strong, tall conifer.

That night I woke up in a red-hot panic from a vivid dream. I felt around for my flashlight, turned it on, propped myself up on one elbow, and began to write:

> *A blood-stigmata erupted in bright red beads along the outside of my right leg. The stigmata snaked from hip to ankle like a sanguine tattoo. Then a priest appeared, swinging a thurible cup back and forth on a chain. Incense billowed up and filled the dreamscape. I held my breath, pulled myself through the stifling air, and rose above the smoke at the last moment before I choked to death. I woke up, gasping for breath.*

I closed my journal and gazed up at a curved sliver of moon dangling in the dark sky, the moon the Sufis call "the thumbnail of God."

Stigmata. It was an esoteric word I hadn't thought of in years, one reserved for those who miraculously experienced crucifixion wounds on their hands and feet. I thought of the legend of Saint Francis of Assisi, the patron saint of animals and the environment, and the first saint to experience stigmata while fasting and praying on a mountain in Italy. Unlike other saints with their halos and pious faces, Saint Francis was portrayed surrounded by birds, rabbits, deer, and snakes at his feet, making him appear more human and friendly. I thought back to my past encounters with snakes, especially the rare sighting of the copulating rattlesnakes tumbling down over the trail on that backpacking trip with Rich. I smiled at the thought that the stigmata dream instilled a magical idea that I'd been anointed with snake medicine, like the statue of Mary, a shamanic snake woman. I rolled to my side, pulled the sleeping bag up under my chin, and eventually fell asleep with images of saints, snakes, and sacraments floating through my mind.

The next morning, I opened my eyes to bright daylight. I'd overslept. Questers were due back at the threshold circle at dawn, and the sun was already well up over the eastern horizon. I threw off my sleeping bag, tugged my pants and bloodstained shirt over my long underwear, and draped my spirit-pouch necklaces over my head. I stuffed my water bottle, sun hat, shawl, journal, and pen into my day pack, hefted it onto my shoulders, and headed for base camp.

A squawking raven broke through the quiet morning as I hurried down the road. *Kraa-caw! Kraa-caw! Kraa-caw! Hurry! Hurry! Hurry!* I hoped I wasn't the last quester to come back to the threshold circle. I didn't want Anne and the others to think I was a slacker. On past quests, I'd been the first to return at dawn. But nothing about this quest was like before—the coffee, chocolate, and wine; the nosebleed and the dream. I thought of Anne's words from years earlier: "You get what you *need* on a quest, not always what you think you want."

Anne was stirring a pot in the camp kitchen when I arrived back at base camp. I set my pack down, brushed the hair from my face, took my place at the edge of the threshold circle, and waited. The raven circled overhead and let out one last *Kraa-caw!* Metal utensils tapped and scraped on bowls from the camp kitchen where the other questers were already enjoying the traditional welcome-back breakfast of potatoes and boiled eggs. Anne laid down the spoon, wiped her hands on a towel, and walked toward me. I was the last quester back.

"Welcome back, dear GG," she said, smiling. Unaware I'd been holding my breath, I exhaled with a sigh.

Anne smudged sage smoke over me; brushed the feather lightly on my forehead, then one cheek, then the other; and finished the feather blessing at my heart. Tears welled up as I received the feather smudging. The movement of the blessing was the same as the Catholic sign-of-the-cross anointing: up, down, and side to side. Anne appeared saintly in the morning light, a warm glow in her eyes. I hoped, when I confessed my questing sins in the story council, she would forgive my transgressions and grant me absolution.

Later, well-fed and rested, I brought my chair to the clearing and settled in with the other questers for the story council. I looked around at the women's disheveled hair and wrinkled, dirty clothes. Their appearances showed wear, but their faces looked relaxed, more open, less tense. They looked transformed. I wondered if I looked different too.

Anne smiled and looked slowly around the circle, making eye contact with each woman and nodding her head in recognition. She then held up the cord of the tingsha bell and bounced the two brass disks together three times. *Ping. Ping. Ping.* She waited for the resonation of the bell to fall completely silent before welcoming us back.

Anne gave us a brief update on how things had been in base camp while we'd been gone. She had seen a few deer, enjoyed quiet communion with the giant ponderosa pine trees, drummed and prayed for us at the threshold circle every morning and evening. On the morning we had left for our solo time, we each put something at our place in the circle—a watch, a pendant, a favorite shell or rock—an item Anne would pick up and hold while she prayed for us. She told us how she'd pick up each item, remember our intention, and speak a prayer on our behalf. I pictured Anne holding the silver, feather-shaped earrings I'd left on a rock at the threshold circle. Perhaps one of her prayers had brought a turning point during my solo time.

"Story council is open," Anne said. "When you feel called to speak, please choose a talking piece and begin."

My pulse quickened. I would speak first and get it over with. I had no idea what I would say, only that I would tell the truth.

I surveyed the choices of talking pieces on the center altar: a shell, a rock, and a small Gaia statue. I went to my knees, reached across the buckskin altar cloth, and picked up the curvy carved stone Gaia. I rested back in the chair, pushed my feet into the ground, squeezed the statue in my hand, and inhaled deeply.

"I'm ashamed to say this," I said, "but I need to confess right off that the only thing I fasted from on this quest were the rules." I kept my eyes riveted to a pinecone on the ground and continued. "I ate chocolate and drank coffee and red wine. I guess you could say, in a way, with the alcohol, that my time was spiritual."

Stifled giggles bubbled up around the circle. Shame washed over me in a hot flush. Would Anne reprimand me in front of everyone?

"I broke the rules," I said. I was on a roll and wanted to get it all out. "I knew I wasn't following the protocols, but it felt good. I wanted—needed—to rebel against it all." I traced my fingers along the Gaia statue in my hand and kept speaking. "I didn't want to come on this quest," I said. "And, after I got here, I wanted to leave."

I shared the nosebleed story, my ritual with the blood-stained water, and the intriguing snake stigmata dream. When I finished, I wiped my tears, placed the Gaia statue back on the altar, clasped my hands together in my lap, and waited for Anne's response. The truth was out. *Here it comes.*

Anne tilted her head, removed her sunglasses, and squinted into the distance. Her feather earrings fluttered lightly in the air. My insides roiled. I lowered my eyes and looked back down at the pinecone. What was she thinking?

"First, there is no right way to quest," she said. "The guidelines I've shared are not rules, they're suggestions. The quest is yours to do in whatever way you choose."

I let out an audible breath. "Really?" I asked. "Is that really true?"

"Yes," Anne said. "Absolutely." She closed her eyes for a few seconds, then opened them and met mine straight on. "I think your experience out there was about much more than just this quest, GG. It's a mirror of your life, your passion, your blood. You took charge of your own experience and did things your own way. You prayed your own way, and that is the teaching."

I began quickly scribbling what Anne said in my journal. But trying to capture her words was a distraction, and I wanted to hear everything she said. So I put my pen down, looked up, and listened.

"You faced your demons," she said. "Embrace them; welcome them. They brought you the rich dream. You didn't want to come on the quest, but you did. When you got here, you didn't want to stay, but you did. Your higher knowing brought you here and kept you here. Your time on Mother Earth brought you what you needed." She stopped speaking, leaned forward, and raised her eyebrows, as if to say, "Understood?"

"You have all the answers inside you," she said. "Don't try to analyze it or figure it out. Just let it be. In time, you'll understand more what happened out there."

I held Anne's gaze and took in her words. *You have all the answers inside you. Let it be.*

When all the questers' stories were told, we finished the council and moved to the threshold circle for the closing ceremony. Each of us expressed our gratitude, to one another and to Mother Earth for her gifts and insights. I picked up my silver feather earrings, held them to my heart, felt the support of the earth beneath my feet and the burden of guilt lift off my shoulders.

"I am thankful to Mother Earth and to my rebelliousness for helping me begin to release the anger and resentment I've been holding that have kept me from living with a more open heart."

On the drive home, I ruminated on Anne's wisdom. She was the wise spiritual guide I'd never had as a child, a compassionate elder who held space without judgment for whatever needed to happen on my quest. She was like Mother Mary, not one of the rigid nuns who had humiliated me and thumped me on the head for breaking rules. Anne was a mirror, and her feedback was a clear reflection of myself and my own experience. I was the one who had gone on the quest. I was the one who made a sacrament from my nosebleed. I was the one who had the snake stigmata dream. I was the one finding my own way.

In the story council circle, I had asked Anne about the snake dream, and she answered my question with a question, "What do snakes mean to *you*?"

"Well . . . snakes get a bad rap," I said. "They crawl on the earth, quietly, taking things in with their tongues. They're grounded in Earth energy. They're mysterious, exotic, and miraculous because they shed their skin and get born anew every year."

As soon as the words came out, I realized it was a description of the experience I'd just had. "I guess that's what I do on my quests too," I said. "I go out on the earth and shed what's no longer needed, like an outgrown skin. I return from my solo time reborn, and sometimes a little bloodstained."

Back home, I unpacked my gear and put everything away. I lit a fire in the fireplace and burned the empty wine boxes and candy wrappers. All the forbidden things I thought were contraband at the outset of my quest had become pathways to my transformation.

"Goodbye, guilt," I said, tossing them into the flames and watching them shrivel and burn. "I am making my own spiritual rules now." I reached in my duffel bag and retrieved the beaded Huichol snake, then walked to my bedroom, placed the snake on my altar, and hung my spirit pouches back on their hook.

I opened a dresser drawer, pulled out a bundle, and unwrapped a ceramic Hummel statue of Saint Francis. The figure wore a brown hooded monk's robe. A fringe of cinnamon-colored hair circled his bald head and matched a tidy red-brown beard. A scarlet bird perched on his arm. His other hand raised up with an open palm facing outward in an all-is-well gesture. At the bottom of the statue on one side of Saint Francis sat a honey-colored rabbit, and a red-and-black-striped snake curled at his feet. The statue had sat on a shelf in my childhood home. Now it would be part of my own altar.

I thought back to the strange yet perfect events that had occurred on my quest. I had broken the rules and relived memories of shame and guilt. I had turned my bloody nose into a healing ceremony. I had found my reconnection to Spirit. Nature was my church. Wilderness questing had become my religion. *Mea vita, mea vita, mea maxima sacra vita.* My life, my life, my most sacred life.

SLEEPING WITH DEATH

Before us great Death stands/ Our fate
held close within his quiet hands. . . .
—Rainer Maria Rilke

Tucked under my pillow was a feather, a lovely specimen
with brown-and-white bands, nine or ten inches long. The
size and shape were that of a bird of prey. I had walked the
circle around my Modoc forest questing site every day but
hadn't noticed the feather until the third day. If it had been
there the whole time, I had missed it. Or it had dropped shortly
before I found it. Maybe it was a wing feather from one of
the hawks that had led me to my power site. I awoke on the
last morning of my solo time to a blanket of silvery frost over
everything in the meadow, including my sleeping bag. Dark
contours of jagged-edged junipers lined up along the morning
horizon, backlit by the rising sun. I shivered, tucked the feather
back under the pillow, and pulled the covers up over my head.

Anne often shared a quote from Stephen Foster, the
author of *The Book of the Vision Quest*: "Don't expect an eagle

to come and land in your power place while you're questing. It's not going to happen." I understood that, but I was
hoping that something would happen. Anything. Finding
the feather that day was a good omen, especially if it had
belonged to a hawk. Ancient myths and stories named the
hawk the messenger bird. *Whenever the hawk shows up, it's
time to pay attention; there is a message coming.* But after four
days, nothing had come.

I stayed tight in my cocoon until the sun rose high
over the horizon and cast a melting warmth that turned the
meadow dewy green. Today I would return to base camp from
my solo time with no story to tell. Something meaningful
had happened on all my other wilderness quests, but this one
had been remarkably unremarkable. I slipped out of my bag
and quickly pulled on my pants and down jacket. Nearby, a
spiderweb hung between two low sage branches and sparkled
in the morning dew. "Well, here's something that happened
overnight," I said, bending down to get a closer look at the
web. Its delicate threads spiraled outward like the spokes of
a wheel and sagged under the weight of shimmering water
beads. It was an exquisite, functional work of art, like a tale
of stories woven together.

One week earlier, I pulled out of the driveway at sunrise and
did a quick mental check: doors locked, light timers set, heat
turned off, garage door closed. I double-checked the inven-
tory for my trip: gear bag packed, tent stowed, sleeping bag
and pad loaded, backpack, food, and water. Then I took a sip
of water from a full bottle and returned it to the cup holder.
Once, I hadn't taken in enough water on a quest and suffered
a raging headache for a couple of days. This time I'd get a
head start on my fluid intake. I'd come a long way since those

early days, learned from my mistakes. Although, each time I ventured out, I never knew what was in store.

At the gas station on the corner, I pulled up next to the pump. I appreciated the fact that, in Oregon, a station worker still filled your tank. My favorite attendant, Johnny, a short, gnomelike guy, stepped up to my window. Johnny's long beard was tied halfway down with a rubber band. The white beard, along with his wide-set eyes, made him resemble an old goat. Pulled down over his wavy hair was a black stocking cap with an embroidered patch that read GOD'S ARMY.

"Hi there," he said. "Well, the End Times are near, and he will be calling his chosen people soon." His big-toothed, friendly smile was incongruent with the odd greeting, but Johnny knew me and usually offered pearls of biblical wisdom as he filled my tank. Odd as he was, I admired Johnny's dedicated approach to life; he knew his purpose.

"Good to know, Johnny," I said. "That's good to know."

"Fill regular?"

"Yes, please," I said, handing him my credit card.

"It's in the book of Revelation," he said, flipping open the door to the gas tank. "Behold the day of the Lord comes, cruel, with wrath and fierce anger to make the land a desolation and destroy its sinners." Johnny loosened the gas cap and tipped the nozzle in.

"Wow. That's intense," I said, leaning out the open window and smiling back at Johnny.

"What are you up to?" he asked, spying the gear bundles in the back seat. "Looks like you're goin' camping or somethin'."

"Oh, out into the backcountry . . . alone, fasting and praying . . . you know, things like that."

With a slight frown, Johnny stroked his beard with a dirty hand. "Seems like you just did that."

"Last spring. I go out every year. This'll be my seventh trip."

"Sounds like Jesus, forty days and forty nights fastin' in the desert. Satan appeared and tried to tempt him, you know," he warned.

"Yeah, kind of like that, I guess. But hopefully without Satan," I said.

Johnny hung the pump back up, pressed a button, tore off the receipt, and handed it through the window. "You take care out there and don't let the devil get ya."

On the drive through town, I thought about something I'd read: that the quest starts the minute you commit to going. I wondered if Johnny's warning about Satan might somehow weave into my experience. There were parts of questing that were hell at times: the boredom, the loneliness, the hunger. But I hadn't ever considered being in the presence of the devil. I didn't believe in the devil. For me, hell was congested freeways and shopping malls; heaven was spending time on wild land and feeling connected to everything in the natural world.

Rows of tilled brown soil and fields of creamy white meadowfoam bordered the highway on the drive south through the Willamette Valley. Cruising down Interstate 5, I counted nine brown-and-white, sharp-shinned hawks perched on fence posts like guides pointing the way. It was a blue-sky day, and I rolled back the sunroof, set the cruise control, and relaxed back in the driver's seat. In the rearview mirror, I spotted the silver streaks in my hair. I mulled over the idea that I would stop dying it brown and let the gray grow out—a retirement rite of passage, going gray. I could give away my professional garb and live in casual clothes. No more trying to look younger. The idea was growing on me.

Three hours into the journey I stopped at the Minute Market in Merrill for a snack. My shoes stuck to the sticky floor as I entered through the automatic double doors.

Behind the checkout counter, a beefy man wore a camouflage baseball cap that read How's my swearing? Dial 1-(800) F-*# You. I wondered if the store manager knew he wore that hat. In my decades-long human resources management career, it would have been my job to counsel this guy about his choice of hats. But no more. I was free from that responsibility. I thought of what my sister Dea, a recovering alcoholic for over thirty years, said in times like these: "Not my circus. Not my monkey."

Cruising along the junk food aisle, I settled on a bag of pretzels. The surrounding coolers held what appeared to be every brand of microbrew beer ever made. I resisted the temptation to grab a six-pack on my way through. The beer reminded me of the retirement party my coworkers had thrown for me a month earlier. I hadn't wanted a party. I wanted to say my goodbyes quietly and not make a big deal out of leaving. But my assistant, Tara, young and hip and up for a party, had insisted. Everyone had shown up to say good-bye, or maybe for the free food and beer. Either way, I played along and made the obligatory it's-been-great-and-thanks-for-everything speech. In the corner of the bar where they'd had the party was an easel with a large poster that read GG's Bucket List. On the poster my coworkers had written suggestions for how to spend my time after retirement. *Take hikes. Travel. Sleep in. Adopt a cat. Waste time.* No one had written, *Go out on a wilderness quest as a rite of passage into retirement.*

Back in my car, I opened the bag of pretzels, popped one in my mouth, and pulled out onto the open road. The flat silvery water of the Klamath Wildlife Refuge stretched out for miles on both sides of the highway. Red-winged black birds perched on rows of cattails and called out their discordant song, *conk-la-reee´-der—conk-la-reee´-der.*

I was officially retired. In the weeks before my quest, I had felt at loose ends. I'd stayed busy cleaning out closets, working in my garden, and keeping the bird feeders filled. But I knew household projects wouldn't satisfy me for the rest of my life. Although there were disappointing things about reaching the level of vice president, my career had been a big part of my life purpose. I had worked since I was eighteen years old. What would be my purpose in retirement? Yes, I had my art, and it brought great fulfillment, and retirement meant more time with the grandkids. But would I miss the power, leadership, and respect I'd had in my job, being the one in charge, the one who made decisions that affected hundreds of people? Elderly white-haired people are overlooked in our society. But I wasn't invisible when I had a title, authority, and chestnut-brown hair from a box of dye. In the corporate environment, a little silver hair at the temples is a sign of experience, but a full head of gray hair suggests you are old and out of touch.

Now, I had no job, no salary, and no professional identity. But I was on my way to a wilderness quest, an experience that I hoped would help me find what was on the other side of my professional life.

With only one-third of my life left to live, why wouldn't I do my best to live it to the fullest?

I turned on the radio. Leonard Cohen's low, simmering voice oozed out a song about a bird on a wire and a drunk in a midnight choir. It took me back to the health evaluation form I had completed at my last physical exam. The slim, perfectly postured doctor sat on a rolling stool across the room. She scanned my answers, page after page, then stopped at one question: *How many glasses of alcohol do you consume per day?* I had filled in the box: *2–3 glasses of wine.*

The doctor took off her glasses and tucked them into the front pocket of her crisp white coat. Her eyebrows slipped down into a frown.

"Two or three glasses of wine a day?" she asked.

"Yes," I said, my arms folded tight across the blue-and-white cotton hospital gown. It was a lie. More like four, sometimes five, enough that I fell asleep on the couch most nights.

She put the questionnaire down and went on with the physical exam: eyes, ears, throat, lungs, and heart.

"You might want to be careful about alcohol," she said as she pressed her fingers over my breasts, checking for lumps. "It's not uncommon for people who retire to become alcoholics. All that free time at home can lead to more drinking."

I thought about my doctor's warning as I drove along the curvy road shoving pretzels into my mouth. It wasn't a good sign that I had lied about how much I was drinking; it was dangerous territory and brought up unpleasant memories. My father had struggled with alcohol his whole adult life. He was sober for a few years, then drunk for several more, then sober, then drunk, and on it went. At family gatherings my brother had followed in my father's footsteps and downed boilermakers, one after another—a shot of whiskey, a glass of beer—until he went red-faced and sloppy and passed out. Before she got sober, one of my older sisters had gone through years of reckless partying that nearly destroyed her relationship with her children. My son was in recovery from drug and alcohol abuse. My mother drank highballs every evening and yet was thriving in her midnineties.

We were a family of alcoholics. And I was on my way. Each day in the late afternoon, I'd start checking the time, figuring out how long before happy hour. Whenever I traveled, I strategized on how and where I would find wine, oftentimes taking it with me to make sure I'd have some. I loved drinking red wine. Without the routine of working, I wondered how long before I'd start drinking at noon. I hated the thought of giving it up but worried that I might follow in my family's footsteps.

Bird-watchers, equipped with binoculars and spotting scopes, filled the roadside turnouts as I drove. I found an open spot, pulled in, and turned off the engine. A single red-tailed hawk rode the warm air currents up and over rocky cliffs, swept up and free. I was free now too, free to do whatever I wanted. Bird-watching might be a fun pastime in retirement—something to keep me occupied, out of the house, and away from wine. I loved birds. I could start a life list like the birders do, recording every bird I saw. A flock of starlings moved in synchronized motion across the sky, drawing together into a thin line, then twisting back out into a wild bulge. They flew in perfect harmony like one organism in a murmuration. The flight pattern was a defense mechanism to confuse predators—each bird copied the movements of the birds that surrounded it to avoid ending up alone and vulnerable at the edge of the flock.

Despite their gallant efforts, the avian strategy didn't work this time. I watched as the dark boomerang shape pivoted mid-flight and dove toward the flock, scattering birds in all directions. The hawk veered off with a small dark lump hanging from its talons. It was a dramatic spectacle, both beautiful and tragic. *Life is paradoxical*, I thought. Retirement promised freedom but also came with a dilemma of how to fill empty days with meaning and purpose.

An hour later I arrived at the Modoc National Forest and turned in on a red-pumice road that led to our base camp on a small rise beneath a huge old-growth juniper tree. I parked my car with the others, stepped out into the fresh air, pulled my arms up over my head, and stretched out the kinks. I found a camping spot several hundred yards from base camp on a rocky outcropping surrounded by mountain mahogany and pine trees. I unloaded my gear and pitched my tent. Finished with camp setup, I grabbed my folding chair, water bottle, journal, and pen and headed out to join the other questers for the opening meeting.

I greeted and hugged "the Wild Hearts," a group of eight women from Southern Oregon with whom I had quested annually for six years. The women looked ready for an outdoor adventure in their Patagonia T-shirts, shorts, brimmed caps, and hiking boots. I unfolded my camp chair, sat down, and kicked off my shoes. The forest duff felt good on my bare feet. The dirt in the Modoc was what I thought of as clean dirt, dry and aromatic and full of disintegrated juniper and pine needles.

Anne passed the smudge bowl, and we took turns cleansing ourselves with sage smoke. She picked up the tingsha bells and bounced them together. A renegade brown curl tumbled onto her forehead. "The circle is open," she said. "Who would like to go first and declare their quest intention?" As usual, my heart beat double time. So much had gone through my mind on the drive to the Modoc: transitioning into retirement, fears about drinking too much. I picked up the talking piece, a ten-inch dried cholla cactus branch polished from years of handling and holding.

"I just retired after forty-five years of working," I said. "My intention for this quest is to release my career identity and be open to what comes next . . . whatever that is." I swallowed back tears. "My career has been a big part of my identity. I'm not sure who I am without it. I know I should be grateful that I can stop working, but I'm a little afraid too." It was a relief to share my trepidation out loud.

That afternoon, we all went our separate ways to find the place we would be for the four-day fast. I ambled through the grass and sagebrush of the Modoc chaparral, scanning the terrain for possible solo sites. I remembered what I had learned about choosing a place. You find a place that feels right, ask permission to quest from the other beings who live there, and listen or watch for a response. There were practical things to think about, too, when choosing a site, like accessibility, safety, and enough seclusion to avoid interruptions by hikers or hunters.

I shaded my eyes and faced west. A red-tailed hawk flew in cursive loops over a nearby meadow, its red-orange tail feathers catching the light as it veered. I recognized the blocky shape, chunky wings, and fan-shaped tail. In bird lore, red-tailed hawks are symbols of truth and higher calling. The raptor called out a piercing scream. A second hawk responded, flew out of a juniper, and joined its mate. I watched the two hawks soar in an aerial ballet, weaving an invisible feathered web through the sky. They continued to call out, as if they were beckoning me. I had questioned the message of one hawk, but seeing two was too auspicious to ignore. I entered the meadow and closed my eyes. "May I spend a few days in this place for my wilderness quest?" I asked. "I promise to be respectful and grateful for all the life here." I waited. All was quiet and calm, and I felt that way too. I took the peacefulness as a *yes* and claimed the meadow below the soaring hawks as the place for my wilderness quest.

A wizened old juniper tree with scooping, craggy limbs bordered one side of my newly chosen site. On the other side lay the skeleton of a fallen juniper comrade with washed-out, broken branches. My questing place sat in between these two monikers of life and death. I hiked back to the road and tied a red bandanna to a tree limb as a location flag, then headed back to base camp. The next morning, my good friend Susanne and I packed up our gear and drove north along the ruddy road to our solo sites. Susanne's wavy gray hair, tied back with a bandanna, bounced up and down as she maneuvered the truck around small bushes and over potholes. I rode quietly in the passenger seat and stared at the road ahead. On past wilderness quests, I had carried everything out and back. At age sixty-five, with a nagging backache and less strength and stamina, I could no longer pack thirty-five pounds a mile and a half back to base camp after a four-day fast.

The loss of strength saddened me. My physical ability was waning right when my emotional and spiritual growth was blossoming. I was at the crossroads where the sloping line of body strength met the upward curve of understanding myself. I hoped the quest would help me come to terms with that junction and surrender gracefully into the transitions that aging inevitably brings, including retirement.

Susanne stopped the truck and looked over at me. She smiled and raised her eyebrows above her glasses. "Is this close enough to your spot?" she asked. We had been questing together for years, and on this quest, we would once again be stone-pile buddies. On past quests we had left gifts for one another at the stone pile, like small works of art and notes of encouragement. Susanne's steadfast nature and easy smile were a comfort to me on a quest. She was a wise and capable outdoors woman.

"Close enough," I said. I hopped out, unlatched the tail-gate, and jumped back as it slammed down with a groan. I unloaded and stacked everything in the brush at the side of the road. My pack was heavy and strained my already aching back, but I was determined to carry it the short distance to my questing site. The straps bit my shoulders as I adjusted the load. Susanne grabbed my gear sack and sleeping bag, and we walked up the rise to the meadow's edge. She needed to know exactly where I'd be in case of an emergency. I pointed across the terrain. "That's my spot between that big juniper on the left and that bleached-out dead tree stump with the clawlike shards sticking up on the right," I said. "Two red-tailed hawks led me here. I trust their guidance."

We set my gear down, and I followed Susanne back over the hill and down the dirt road. She showed me her questing place, then we said our goodbyes and made plans to meet at the stone pile four days later. I returned to my spot in the grassy meadow. Clumps of yellow desert parsley scattered in foamy pools across the prairie like puddles of sunshine. Meadowlarks trilled cheerful songs. I stood and breathed in the wildflowers, the birdsongs, and the peaceful wild. This would be my humble home for the next four days.

I had read that Indigenous people undertook their wilderness quests in small, confined areas. The seeker stayed isolated for as long as it took to achieve the desired goal, up to three or four days, then emerged with a vision. On past quests, I had walked, climbed, and explored. This time I would try to stay within a defined circle. It would be challenging, but my choice was more instinctual than rational. I was surrendering into limitation, turning into the skid, and following the lead of the native Modoc people with the idea that confinement might somehow lead to deeper insight.

I collected dry limbs and crafted them into a wide circle beginning at the base of the old juniper. I pried black pumice rocks from the dirt and placed them between the limbs in a repeated pattern: rocks and limbs, rocks and limbs. The dark pumice and bone-colored branches extended from the foot of the juniper tree like a fifty-foot black-and-white necklace. I stood back and admired my creation. I had done this before. On my first quest I'd made a Medicine Wheel protection circle to sleep in. And on my fifth wilderness quest, a purpose-circle nest. This time I had defined the small space I would live in for four days.

The next morning brought a crisp, cold dawn. I rolled onto my back, pulled the down cover in close, and watched clouds puff up and dissipate into webbed strings across the sky. I had an entire day ahead of me, an entire day of nothing.

Much of that day I sat in my chair, my mind adrift. My legs stiffened and my back tightened. I got up and walked my circle, scouting for feathers, bones, animal scat, anything of interest. Finding nothing, I sat back down.

The two trees on either side of me mirrored my own restlessness—up and alive and moving through space like the green juniper boughs, then down and quiet and stagnant like their dead companion, like the hawk and the starlings I'd seen on the drive in. *Life and death. That's what it comes down to. Get busy living or get busy dying.* But I had nothing to get busy doing out there in the Modoc. My pattern of movement and quiet went on until sun met moon. At dusk I crawled back into my sleeping bag. A conspiracy of ravens glided stealthily overhead, evenly spaced, wingbeats in sync. Their blue-black feathers sliced the air like paddles moving through dark water, leaving a *whooshing* sound in their wake, as if they were on an important mission with somewhere to go and something to do.

Darkness set in. Owls called to one another across the chaparral. Coyotes wailed in sharp barks that ended in long, drawn-out, quavering howls. Amplified by the darkness, the moaning sounds gave me the shivers. There were times on my quests when I was still afraid of the dark. I told myself I was safe, that my fears were all in my head, but my physical body told a different story. I trembled at the core, terrified. I knew it wasn't rational. Coyotes don't harm humans; in fact, they want nothing to do with us and will usually turn and run at first sight. Still, regardless of the many times I'd heard coyotes howling on other quests, for some reason this time, my heart pounded with fear. Spurts of adrenaline flushed through my body. My mind said there was no danger. My body said run like hell.

The disconnect between my mind and body wasn't all that different from the way I had responded to the idea of retirement. I intellectually rationalized that retirement was something good—I had my art hobby, was financially secure, and welcomed more free time. Still, I knew the fears I had about retirement were manifesting in my physical body in ways I couldn't control. My lower back, the place in my body that went into spasms when I was under stress, had been painful for the last few weeks.

There were times, growing up with an alcoholic father and a mother who stuffed down her anger, when I carried all the sadness and rage for the entire family. A part of me felt that same childhood vulnerability and insecurity, though there was no real danger in the moment. The body keeps score, and my back hurt. I had learned from years of bouts with back pain that a good cry helped. So I turned my full attention to the mushy ache in my chest and the spasmodic clenching in my back and had myself a good cry. The Milky Way cast a twinkling swath over the night sky. The coyotes quieted down. The only sound was my sniffling and the occasional *peent-peent* cries of nighthawks diving for insects in the darkness.

Over the four days of solo time, I slogged through more hours of repetition: sit, watch the clouds, sketch, write in my journal, stretch my sore back, get up and walk around, pee, drink water, sit down again, get up and walk again, then go to bed at the end of the day. I knew firsthand that wilderness questing was mostly waiting and watching and often boring. At times I vowed never to put myself through it again. On this quest, I wanted it to be over. And I wanted my back spasm to release, but it stayed tight. I wanted something exciting to happen on my wilderness quest too, but so far that wasn't happening either.

At home, when I had been working, I'd had a busy routine: morning exercise, a one-hour commute, a full workday, home, wine, dinner, television, and bed. Weekends were spent on domestic chores and outdoor activities. Out here in the wilderness, there was no commute and no workday. I forced myself to sit down in my circle, be quiet, and feel the pain and restlessness. I sat with all my questions: Is this what retirement would be like? Would I be bored out of my gourd? What was I afraid of? At that moment, I might have killed for a glass of wine.

Throughout my life, there had been new rites of passage: menstruation, driver's license, losing my virginity, marriage, childbirth, completing my education, my first professional job, buying a home, and my promotion to corporate vice president. Everything moved toward expansion and advancement.

I feared the reversal of that process. One by one, things would go away as I got older. I'd seen it happen with my mother. First menopause and retirement. Then your license is taken away. Eventually you can't take care of business, so family members step in. There comes a time when you can't attend to your personal needs, and someone brings you food, helps you dress, and changes the sheets on your bed. You lose track of what day it is, what you had for breakfast, and your daughter's name. I'd been independent—had grown up with little adult supervision, married young, divorced young, and taken care of things on my own. I'd learned through the years that the only person I could totally count on was myself. The thought of losing my independence terrified me even more than the howling coyotes.

There is a passage in a poem by Rainer Maria Rilke: *Be patient toward all that is unsolved in your heart and try to love the questions themselves.* But I didn't love all my unanswered questions. I got out my journal and wrote. Had I retired too soon? What was my life purpose without my career? What was my identity without my professional status? Was retirement the beginning of the end? I left all the questions in my journal unanswered and tucked it back into my pack, then stretched out for more mindless cloud watching. My solo fasting time had been terribly uneventful. All I really had to show for time in the meadow was an aching back and a list of unanswered questions.

On that last morning, when I pulled the hawk feather back out from under my pillow, I looked out over the frosty meadow and resigned myself to going back to base camp that day without a story to tell. I was sure it had happened to others too. It was not the end of the world. I tucked the brown-and-white feather above my ear and started to deflate my mattress the way I always did, down on my knees and squeezing the air out as I rolled. A movement caught my eye. From somewhere in or around my bedroll, a shiny black object the size of a blueberry tumbled out, bounced over my knee, and landed on the tarp next to me. I gasped and jerked away. I knew instantly what that distinct, shiny, bulbous shape was. Cold and stiff, she lay there on her back, barely moving, slowly curling her pointed legs in the air like sharp, witchy fingernails. A tiny red hourglass emblazoned her abdomen. Bilateral mandibles as sharp as needles jutted out from below her head. There was no mistaking who she was—a creature with a bite fifteen times more toxic than a rattlesnake—a black widow spider. A chill surged through me. I realized, in horror, that she'd been in bed with me. I expected her to flip herself over and skitter away. But the morning air was near freezing and too cold for crawling. I felt cold and paralyzed too, seeing her lying there so close beside me.

My first inclination was to smash her with my foot. But why kill a creature natural to this area? The spider was beautiful in a horrific way, her shiny carbon-black body in contrast with the lipstick-red hourglass. Did she deserve to die just because she was poisonous and could have bitten me? But she hadn't bitten me. No. I would not kill her. This was her world. I was the intruder. I scooped her up gently with my handkerchief and released her in a clump of grass.

She tumbled and landed under a crisscross of green stems. I wondered how close I had come to being bitten. If I had been bitten, would I have been able to walk toward Susanne's spot and yell for help? Would I have felt the bite? Or would I have died in my sleep? If I'd slept with the black widow, and she hadn't bitten me, and I hadn't squished her in my sleep, there must have been a reason we were both still alive. I knew I'd meet death someday, hopefully sometime long into the future. I didn't know when that black curtain would come down on me, or how I would be delivered across that threshold. Thankfully, it wasn't destined to happen on my seventh wilderness quest.

There was so much of life ahead of me, so many things to do and see. I wanted to go to Costa Rica, revisit the Southwest, and kayak in mountain lakes. I thought of a litany of other things I wanted to accomplish, like writing a book about my wilderness questing. Retirement did not mean the end of living a purposeful life. It did, however, mean the end of my wine habit. Reflecting on the history of alcoholism in my family while I was out there, and considering my tendency to overdo, I vowed to give up the red wine that I loved so much. Pack on my back, I headed down the road to meet Susanne for the ride back to base camp. Despite four days of fasting, my load felt lighter. My lumbar muscles had let go, and my back felt better. I had a bounce in my step. I was alive, and I had a story to tell.

No eagle had landed in my power place, but the red-tailed hawks had led me to a clearing between the two junipers, monikers of life and death. And something tiny, powerful, and dangerous had crept in and brought with her a clear message: get busy living; death could come crawling out from under the mattress at any moment.

Top, *Ancestors of the Four Directions*; Bottom, *Gift from Rock Spirits*

Top, *Bird Whisperer*; Bottom, *Deeper Discoveries*

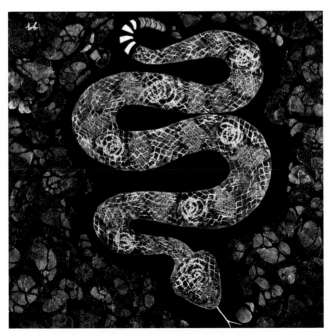

Top, *Grandmother Spirits in My Garden*;
Bottom, *Rattled Awakening*

Left, *Shamanic Snake Woman*;
Right, *The Kiss Withheld*

Top, *Dark Spirits Under Starry Skies*;
Bottom, *Coyote Wild*

Left, *Land Kintsugi*;
Right, *The Trickster* (inspired by Rebecca Haines, artist)

Top, *Being Held in Deep Grief and Unbearable Beauty*; Bottom, *July Full Buck Moon*

Finding My Voice

SMALL THINGS
DIE EVERY DAY

The breeze at dawn has secrets to
tell you. Don't go back to sleep.
—Rumi

Stuck in a tent during an unrelenting downpour for forty-eight hours, all I wanted was for the rain to stop so I could escape from the small confined space. Rivulets of water had streamed down the outside walls, pooled along the ground tarp, and bled dark bronze around the tent floor. I wondered how long before that damp seeped into every fold and recess of my sleeping bag and, eventually, me.

An experienced wilderness quester, I knew that May weather in the Modoc was unpredictable. Once it had snowed a few inches. But this was the first time I'd been trapped in a two-person (more like one person and a duffel bag) tent for so long. My back and hips hurt. My patience had worn thin.

Before the quest, I had imagined how the days might unfold. I would meander over the chaparral, then sit in quiet solitude and watch the sky change color, listen to bird calls. I had announced these plans in the circle council three days earlier: "My intention is to be present with nature, watch closely, and be open to the teachings that the land offers." Unlike my previous quests, I didn't have a specific trauma or issue to address. I wanted to receive whatever came.

The morning after my two-day confinement in the downpour, I woke up to a light wind ruffling the nylon and an intense desire for fresh air. I went to unzip my tent door, but the nylon fabric wadded in the zipper. "Damn it," I said, yanking at the metal pull. With some finagling up, down, and up again, it gave way. I crawled out of the opening, stood up, and stretched tall. I breathed in wet earth and juniper air and blessed quiet. Spring in the Modoc was alive with wildflowers and verdant new growth. A meadowlark on the ridge above me erupted in a melodious trill. Shards of light radiated from the pewter sky like those in religious paintings, signaling hope for a sunny day. Liberation at last. I was free from the four orange walls of that tent. I surveyed my camp for damage from the two-day downpour. I was pleased that the tarp I'd tied in the lower boughs of the juniper had held well. The prayer pouches I had made—thirteen small fabric bundles filled with tobacco and questing prayers and tied closed at the ends—hung drenched and sagging from a line of yarn that stretched between two juniper trees. My camp chair and gear bag were damp from slanted rain, but not soaked. The moss on the rocks had turned a deep lush green. Where I had trudged carelessly before, I now chose my footfalls to avoid the velvet mat, aware of how fresh and alive everything appeared after the rain.

I couldn't wait to set out on a walkabout to quiet my busy mind and restless body. I searched for signs of life: animal tracks, an owl feather, or an arrowhead. It was part of my ceremony—looking for signs and symbols from nature and letting them guide me toward new insights. Meandering along a dirt road that ran north and south through the chaparral, I crested a small hill and stopped. Ahead, something thin and curved lay inert on the graveled shoulder. I stepped closer.

When my son, Bill, was young, we read from his favorite book, *Peterson's Field Guide to Western Reptiles and Amphibians*. Night after night, we studied the names of all the reptiles and gazed at the color photographs. I was as intrigued as Bill was by the descriptions and characteristics of each snake, frog, newt, and salamander. That's how I recognized the brown-and-black-hexagon pattern on the creature lying in the road. It was a baby gopher snake that appeared to be dead. I touched it with my finger. It felt cold, but not stiff, with no sign of injury. I felt a distant calling, like a wordless voice. I remembered the beaded snake that held my place in the medicine bundle and marveled at the auspicious coincidence.

During the circle council, we had performed the ritual opening of the medicine bundle—a bread-loaf-sized tied leather sheath that held a personal spiritual totem from each of us. The bundle represented the power of a loving and supportive community, our eclectic version of a family crest, and we took turns taking it home with us after each quest. Whoever needed extra energy in the coming days would keep the bundle for strength and courage, then return it at our next meeting.

When Anne opened the bundle at the beginning of council circle, she offered gratitude to the North American tribal members who had held on to the teaching of ceremonial medicine bundles. One of the Wild Hearts, Holly, a research librarian, had also shared that most people think medicine bundles were only used by the native tribes of North America, but they were also discovered in other cultures dating back ten thousand years based on remains found in the Swiss Alps and on ancient murals discovered in Turkey. I felt honored to participate in this sacred and enduring ritual. The small Huichol beaded snake I had contributed was there in the opened bundle, along with the other questers' items: a black onyx bear fetish, a heart-shaped rock, a tiny yarn doll, an exotic-looking green feather, a miniature book of poems, a cluster of white sage, an egg-shaped rattle, obsidian chips, and an aquamarine crystal that looked like a piece of petrified ocean. The bundle stayed open during our circle council to let our power juju radiate out around our circle and into the world. At the meeting's end, we rewrapped the bundle, tied it with a cord around the outside like a package, and tucked it under a juniper tree.

I had quested in the Modoc seven times before, but on that trip, I felt the presence of the Moatokni maklak ancestors, the Modoc people who had inhabited the land for thousands of years before Euro-American fur trappers came to the area in the early 1800s. The Modoc, the Pit River or Achomawi, and the Northern Paiute tribes still occupy the area today. Lying in my tent the night before, halfway between sleep and consciousness, I had heard a voice say, "Let go and trust." I blinked awake and wondered if it had been an actual person speaking or a voice in a dream. Was I going crazy from the entrapment? I didn't know what I was being asked to let go of or if I wanted to follow the advice of a nameless voice. Then I remembered that it was important to pay attention to subtle messages, especially on a quest.

How could I learn to let go of control and trust in a greater, universal wisdom?

In Death Valley, I had followed the urge to strip naked, which turned into a spontaneous body-shame healing ritual. In the Inyo Mountains, I responded to the call of the black rock ridge and sat under the lone pine tree for hours reconnecting with my childhood love of art. And here I was on another wilderness quest, looking to nature for signs and omens. *Let go and trust.* What I wanted in that moment, looking at the dead gopher snake, was to pick it up and take it with me. But for what purpose? *Let go and trust.* I scooped up the snake and held it in my hand for a moment. If the creature had any life left, the warmth of my hand might revive it. But there was no movement. The limp body smelled of sage mixed slightly with skunk. I slid it into a plastic bag that I carried for toilet paper waste and slipped the bundle into my pocket.

Up over a rise in the road, I stopped again. This time, it was a dead thumb-sized frog. Black camouflage spots dotted the translucent blue-green skin. The back legs splayed out in a diamond shape. Once again, there was no sign of injury, simply a dead frog. I fished the bag from my pocket and placed the little amphibian in it with the snake. Farther down the road was another dead frog, a twin to the first one, the same blue-green skin, the same black spots. I picked it up and eased it into the bag along with the others.

How odd that I had come looking for signs of life but now had three dead creatures in my pocket. I wondered about the meaning of collecting dead things. It didn't matter what it meant. *Let go and trust.* My intention was to be present with nature, watch closely, and be open to what felt right in the moment.

"Okay, guys," I said, my voice echoing back to me from the open chaparral. "We're going to have a death wake."

Back at my campsite, under the juniper tree, I took out the dead snake and frogs and arranged their wet bodies on a moss-covered lava rock. I placed the snake in the middle, the frogs on either side. Their colors were so vibrant in the overcast skylight that they looked as if they would slither or hop away at any moment. I got down on my belly and looked closely at their lifeless eyes, studying their physical structure. Imagine being in a body that moves over rocks, grass, and water without any legs, scaled skin gliding you forward, smelling the air with your tongue. Or fringed, webbed feet bigger than your head that propel you through water like a torpedo. On land your belly stays in touch with the earth, so close you feel it as part of yourself. You go where your instincts take you without self-consciousness, your only mission to survive.

I'd spent hours on my belly in the dirt at the creek across from my childhood home. That was where I'd learned to find solace in nature and joy in small wild things. I caught tadpoles and frogs, picked blackberries, and stayed cool in that ravine on long sizzling summer afternoons. I once caught a garter snake and kept it in my room in a terrarium with dirt and foliage. To keep it alive, I fed it worms. One day she gave birth to a dozen live babies that slithered in random chaos around the glass walls trying to get out. Neighborhood kids knocked at the door and asked to see the baby snakes.

I was the only kid on the block who had ever owned baby snakes. I wanted to keep them, but my brother convinced me they would die in the overcrowded terrarium. I let them all go, but not before I held them once more and felt their ribbon bodies tickle across my hands and bare legs. I was surprised by this memory and this person I had been so long ago. While my girlfriends would have nothing to do with snakes or frogs, I had loved them and enjoyed the curious feel of their cool, smooth bodies.

Small things die every day, and people don't notice or care. Looking at the snake and frogs lying on their stony tomb like an illustration from a nature journal, I realized they represented things in me that had died when I was small too. My innocence lay inert. My vulnerability splayed out limp. My trust, cold and still.

The year I turned ten was rough. My mother, a devout Catholic who raised us to be the same, divorced my father and was living life as a single woman. The church excommunicated her, punishing her for being divorced instead of celebrating her ability to liberate herself from the trauma and heartache that comes with living with an alcoholic. My sisters, who were eight years older and had been like two extra moms to me, got married in a double wedding ceremony and moved out of the house. My brother, fourteen years old, sank into a deep depression and disappeared into his bedroom lair. I was alone but found respite at the creek.

Wilderness questing was my way of returning to that girl I had once been, the one who loved the land and felt wonder and joy in nature. Feeling her inside me, I plunged into the moment, slathered mud on my face, dangled mossy strings in my hair, shook a rattle, and danced in circles around the dead. When I was all danced out, I sank to my knees and cried for that lonely little girl who was left to find companionship in cold-blooded creatures.

Later that afternoon the sun came out and dried the rain puddles. Flickers whistled sharp calls from the silhouetted branches of a nearby snag. I changed into shorts and flip-flops and soaked in the warmth. The dead frogs changed, too, to a deeper oceanic teal as they shrank and shriveled from the heat. The snake's eyes filmed over and collapsed in. I picked them up and carried them a few hundred yards away to a rocky outcropping where I'd spotted a shallow cave. I arranged the reptiles on the dirt floor of the cave, face-to-face in a triad, and said a prayer of gratitude for the insights the little ones had sparked in me. I stood up, brushed the dirt from my knees, and walked back through the grassy meadow with the image of the three creatures still clear in my consciousness. They would go back to the earth as food for scorpions, centipedes, and ants.

A movement in the brush stopped me. I looked but didn't see anything. I took another step, and a dark shape caught my attention. There in the brush was a four-foot-long, very much alive snake. The chain-like pattern along its back was a giant replica of the pattern on the baby snake I'd left in the cave. The midsection, though, was as big around as my wrist. I scanned the tail. No rattle. It was a gopher snake. It slithered away, as startled perhaps as I was.

"Well, hello there," I said.

The snake stopped. It turned toward me. Grass swished under its body as it slid forward, its forked tongue whipping through the air.

I did not move, barely breathed, as the snake inched closer.

The creature continued toward my exposed feet. It stopped in front of my bare toes, tongue lashing out and back, out and back. A cold chill spread over my skin. Gopher snakes have small sharp teeth, and although they aren't venomous, their bite can be painful. *Let go and trust.* With one last whip, the forked tongue slashed out and brushed my big toe. Then the snake turned and undulated over the ground and disappeared. I stood mesmerized. It felt like a shamanic blessing. I thought of the statue of Mary in my childhood church and the serpent curled at her feet. The feeling of the snake's tongue on my skin stayed with me all the way back to my power site. Back in the tent, I lay on my sleeping bag and relived my one day of freedom: the search for life, the discovery of death, a memory of being a young mother with my son, a child holding snakes before setting them free, the solace of nature, the snake licking at my bare toe.

I took the power bundle home after the quest to keep the experience fresh in my heart and mind. I had never expected torrential rains and being holed up in my tent to the point of near hallucination. But that's how questing in the wild is. You get what you get, then you look for the meaning in it all.

FACING MY FEAR:
Two Girls in
THE MODOC

Our deepest fears are like dragons,
guarding our deepest treasure.
—Rainer Maria Rilke

A low-pitched guttural snort bolted me from sleep. My first thought was the cougar. I rolled onto my back, perked up my ears, and held my breath. Stars glinted in an indigo sky through the mesh tent window overhead. Was I dreaming? The day before I had forged a trail through foxtail weeds and fragrant Modoc sagebrush, searching for a power place. I wanted a spot with a never-ending, uninterrupted view, far away and out of earshot from other people. The warning from Anne hovered at the back of my mind: "Be alert on your solo time. A cougar was recently spotted walking along the south ridge. I'm not trying to scare you, just reminding you to pay attention to what's going on around you."

The area was the perfect habitat for cougars, also called mountain lions, with rocky outcroppings, pockets of thick shrubbery for hiding, and plenty of deer and rabbits to hunt. I wondered how far from base camp it was safe to go and spend four days and nights alone. I ended up in a grassy meadow under a lone juniper tree, a quarter of a mile from base camp. It seemed as safe a place as any. I had trudged back and forth three times that day, carrying my gear: tent, sleeping bag, clothing sack, equipment bag, art supply tote, and four one-gallon water bottles. Even the quarter mile stretched my capacity to carry so much gear. On each trip I stopped halfway out under a pinion pine tree, laid down my load, sat on a rock, took a long drink of water, and rested up for the next round. I considered the potential danger of being out alone day and night where a cougar had been spotted. I would have been both thrilled and terrified to see one.

After I'd hauled out my supply cache, I pulled poles and an orange nylon bundle from the stuff bag and pitched my tent by an old-growth juniper tree laden with aromatic purple berries. Weather reports had shown a 30 percent chance of rain, and after the two-day downpour I'd experienced once before in the Modoc, I wasn't taking any chances. I worked the poles through grommets and loops until I had a four-foot-high dome-like abode sitting under the sprawling limbs. I left the rain fly off to expose the mesh window that stretched across the tent roof but left it nearby in case the sky threatened. Without the rain fly, there would be nothing between me and the stars except a thin mesh screen. I settled into my camp chair and pulled out a bag of art supplies that my questing friend Susanne had given me. It was a treat to poke through someone else's stash of odds and ends—bits of decorative papers, small collage images, ribbons, fabric, embroidery thread, needles, and beads. A wad of purple fabric caught my eye. I unearthed the patterned cotton from the bottom of the bag and spread it out. Clumps of tiny yellow and red flowers with green leaves scattered here and there over the violet cotton, along with images of wild animals— bears, wolves, eagles, horses, and, coincidentally, cougars. I chose one of the cougar images and made myself another spirit pouch, this one with the tan-and-brown cougar on the front and a horse on the back. I filled the new pouch with aromatic juniper berries and hung it from a loop at the top of my tent.

"There," I said. "You've been recognized and honored, Mr. Cougar. Now stay away."

At day's end, the giant sun slid down between wisps of clouds, stopping to rest on the skyline as if reluctant to give up the day. Not yet ready to call it a day myself, I tied my shawl around my shoulders and picked up my drum. Abstract shapes danced across the tie-dyed surface of the drum like symbols from a shamanic dream. I brushed my hand over remnants of horsehair follicles that tickled against my fingers. Playing the drum was a comfort, and I had drummed out my melancholy on its sturdy body many times on past quests.

I began drumming. *Boom—boom—boom!* The warm dry air had pulled the surface tight, and the sound bounded out in a strong, clear bravado. The pounding sent a vibration up my arm and through my heart like a soothing pulse.

I drummed until the sun went down and only a swath of vermilion stretched along the horizon. After hours of tromping back and forth, bringing out my gear, concentrating on my sewing, and drumming, I was beyond exhaustion and collapsed in my tent. Eventually, my restless legs worked themselves out. Stars appeared, one after another, as the night closed in until a sky alive with twinkling sirens lulled me to sleep. I hadn't been asleep for long when I heard the low-pitched guttural snort that awakened me, a noise I couldn't identify. I felt the first rush of fear adrenaline flood my veins.

If it was a cougar, I had no real weapon, only a pocketknife buried somewhere in my pack, which lay out of reach in the far corner of the tent.

Then I heard it again, the sound of air fluttering through lips, *Bbbrrruuuu.* A bucolic scent filled the air, like a barnyard. *That's no cougar,* I thought. *Horses? Really? Out here with nothing but flimsy nylon tent walls to keep me from being stomped to death?* My heart kicked up. A get-ready-to-run signal bull-horned inside my head. The sound and smell bolted me back to a childhood memory.

"Horses are friendly," said Sherry, my best friend and next-door neighbor in the suburban California subdivision where we grew up. Sherry and I were both ten years old. During the summer while our moms worked, we stayed home alone, ate grilled cheese sandwiches, and watched soap operas on TV.

"They're big, but you get used to them," she said. "And my uncle's horses are really nice."

"But I don't know how to ride a horse," I said, quaking at the very idea.

"My uncle will help you. Come on. It will be so fun."

Sherry's uncle Allen turned out to be an eighteen-year-old, dark-haired dreamboat in cowboy boots, jeans, and a chambray shirt. I blushed pink when he placed his hands on my sides and helped me up into the smooth leather saddle and onto a horse named Gertie. I grabbed the saddle horn and spread my legs wide across the coffee-table-sized mid-section of the beast. The horse groaned and grunted.

"You'll be fine," Allen said. "Just hold on." So I did.

Heart in my throat, I white-knuckled the reins. The powerful muscles of the beast's haunches shifted beneath me. The giant coffee-brown head and black mane heaved up and down like the prow of an unanchored ship. I peeked over the side. It was a long way down. I hoped it would be a short ride. Allen helped Sherry onto a mahogany-brown horse, then mounted his white one, and the three of us ambled through the pasture and down a well-worn trail, Gertie and me last in line. I relaxed and was starting to enjoy the ride when Gertie, having fallen behind the other horses, broke into a trot. One thousand pounds of wither and loin heaved under my quivering legs, and I bounced up and down hard against the saddle like a loosely tethered ball. I pulled at the reins like I'd seen in the cowboy movies. "Whoa," I said, "whoa." Gertie paid me no mind. She swerved her giant head back and forth but kept trotting. Her movement pushed the saddle sideways, and I felt my bottom slip precariously. I stopped yanking, regained my place center saddle, and held on. We caught up with the other horses, and thankfully, Gertie slowed down.

"How far are we going?" I yelled.

"Not far," Allen said. "Just through those trees ahead and around the other side of the property, then back to the corral. How are you doing?" he asked.

"Okay," I said, "but I don't know how to steer the horse."

"Just hold on," Allen said. "You don't need to steer. Gertie knows what she's doing."

Sherry smiled back at me. "Isn't this fun?" she asked. I didn't respond.

We meandered through the meadow and on up through the trees. At a turn in the path, Gertie stopped following Sherry's horse and struck out on her own. She ambled off the trail and under the sprawling limbs of an oak tree. She stopped under the tree, lowered her head, and began munching on grass. I held tight to the saddle horn and ducked under the branches. "Come on," I said. "Get moving." I kicked my heels toward her loins, the way those movie cowboys did. Gertie sidled her neck up against the tree trunk and sauntered forward, rubbing her body, and with it my leg, over the bark.

"Help!" I screamed. "Help!" I instinctively pulled my leg back. My balance teetered. I plunged my foot back into the stirrup and anchored myself. I had no choice but to hold on while the ornery horse smashed my bare leg against the rough bark that scraped over my skin and dug into my leg and ankle.

"Ouch! You're a stupid horse," I said, whimpering as I watched blood drip down my leg. Gertie trotted out of the trees and back to her rightful place behind the other horses on the trail like a naughty kid sneaking back in line. Allen rode back to me, took over my reins, and led Gertie and me back to the corral. He helped me dismount and offered an apology for the mishap, which he said had never happened with Gertie before. I sat on the fence with Sherry, picked bark flakes from my bleeding wounds, and swore to myself that I'd stay away from horses forever.

Listening to hard hooves thumping over the ground outside my tent, I lay paralyzed with fear. My back stiffened, and I pressed my elbows to my sides and waited, hoping the horses would leave. But no. Two horses appeared through the tent window like gothic intruders peering down at me. Long oval shapes. Pointed ears. Stars bright in the night sky behind their looming heads. I groped in the tent side pocket, grabbed my flashlight, and snapped it on. A cone-shaped beam shone through the mesh window and revealed how close the horses were, nearly within reach. The light shone over two long sorrel-brown muzzles with gaping black nostrils and eyes that glowed greenish-white under fringed lashes. I unzipped my bag, sat up, ran the light farther down their bodies, and discovered they were mares.

"Shoo, shoo!" I yelled and clapped my hands in repeated pops. "Go away!" They stayed put. One grunted and groaned.

"Go, go!" This time I smacked my hands together faster and louder. I'd been told horses are easily spooked, but not these two. It seemed to pique their interest. One nuzzled at a gear bag I'd left on the ground outside by my tent. I whacked the tent wall. "Get out of there!" I yelled.

The horse raised its head and bumped the juniper limbs, sending a hailstorm of berries down over the top and sides of the tent. My arms shot over my head as if the berries might breech the mesh. The cougar and horse pouch I'd sewn swung back and forth from its anchor point on the tent loop. Was I clairvoyant? Would a cougar come next? I weighed my options: lie there or get up and try to chase them away. My body responded with a sudden and rigid *no*. I didn't think I could leave the false security I felt cuddled inside my sleeping bag, behind the thin nylon wall. Would anyone hear if I called for help? What would I yell? *Help! Two horses are looking at me!* I pressed my hands over my face and froze.

My intention for that quest that year was to find the courage to face the fears that had held me back my whole life: fear of failure, fear of looking foolish, fear of being ridiculed, and fear of rejection. I had expanded my art practice to include calling myself an "art doula," working one-on-one with people and facilitating multiday retreats. The thought of stepping more fully into my role as a teacher gripped me with fear. I felt like a total impostor, and I was not making any progress on a retreat that was coming up soon. Years ago I'd heard or read the advice that the more something scares you, the more you should probably do it. My encounter with the horses was the chance to confront one of my oldest fears head-on.

How could I use this experience to dissolve old fears that were holding me back?

The black shapes stood side by side above me like disquieting sentinels, as if they were waiting for something. The outline of their powerful muscular necks against the night sky, their snorts and sniffs, the sweat, hair, and manure—it was all dreamlike. I stayed put, closed my eyes, and focused on the hard knot in my gut. With my attention there, I took in a deep breath and asked myself if I was really in any danger. Horses aren't predators. These two were big and daunting, yes, but they weren't going to eat me.

I stayed with my breath, and the knot in my gut let go a little. I did a full-body scan, then breathed into each place that felt tight. After several minutes of telling myself I was not in any danger, my heartbeat slowed back to normal, and my clenched jaw relaxed. I adjusted my pillow, brought my arms up, and clasped my hands behind my neck. I settled in and watched the horses watch me. The two horses with their tilted heads, wide-open eyes, and perked-up ears seemed content, like great lurking angels.

One shifted its weight, and a shiver rolled down its head and neck. In the same way that a yawn is contagious, the rippling of horsehair sent a chill down my back and raised the hair on my neck and arms. Somewhere within that massive equine flesh, bone, and sinew beat a heart three times bigger than mine. I couldn't shake the fantastic idea that I may have called the beasts in with my drumming the night before. The drum had held a magical presence from the moment I'd made it years earlier at the home of a medicine woman named Naomi in Mount Shasta City.

The day I showed up for the drum-making class, Naomi greeted me at her door wearing a white buckskin dress with beads, ribbons, and swaying fringe with tiny bells that jingled as she barefooted across the room. I stood in her foyer, mesmerized by the art, drums, and rattles that adorned every bit of available wall space, like artifacts in a museum of Native treasures.

Naomi gathered us in her backyard and guided us through a prayer and sweetgrass smudging ritual. Mount Shasta filled the whole eastern sky over Naomi's backyard, an imposing, omniscient presence. I sat under a gnarled apple tree and rolled the soles of my bare feet over small, hard green apples that covered the ground. I draped the wet horsehide over a maple wood frame, carefully centering the leather over the circle, then pulled it tight and tied the leather lacing the way Naomi had instructed.

My drum had been with me on every quest since that day. I rubbed my fingers over the stretched hide. The horses could have stomped me but showed no aggression, giving me no reason to fear them. They weren't the unpredictable ungulates from my childhood. They seemed docile. Were they domestic, wild, or feral? Why were they out in the middle of nowhere? And why in heck had they come to stand over me?

From somewhere in the recesses of my gray matter, the image of a hexagram from *I Ching: The Chinese Book of Changes* appeared. I knew it well: *Hexagram #2: Relaxing, Flowing, Responsive: The unmoving mover of it all sits in the center, docile as a mare*. I had learned about the I Ching years earlier in a workshop I had taken when I first moved to Salem. The ancient Chinese oracle guide is based on a series of hexagrams that are built by randomly pulling six colored marbles from a bag (or by tossing three coins), then drawing six lines that correlate with the marble color. Each hexagram has a name, like #2, Earth over Earth, also called *The Receptive*. I had experimented with the I Ching over the years and had come up with Hexagram #2 several times. I found out later that the odds of repeating the same hexagram were something like ten thousand to one. Once, I had drawn the marbles that created #2 (six black, all yin energy) on two consecutive readings. I felt there was some correlation between my visitors and the docile mare referred to in Hexagram #2.

I named my nighttime visitors *the Girls*. Two big-hearted, docile creatures standing sentinel over my small orange half-dome tent out in the middle of the Modoc. They stayed—for I don't know how long—watching and waiting. I would close my eyes and doze, then wake up later, and they would still be there. Eventually, I fell asleep between one moment of equine silhouettes and stars and another moment of drifting into darkness. I awoke later to the sounds of more grunting and soft stomping, and it made me laugh out loud.

"You girls are relentless," I said. "Okay. You've won me over. If you want to hang out here, fine, but please don't step on me."

One of the horses made a sound somewhere between a groan and a nicker. I rolled over and drifted back into sleep. Sometime in the wee hours I awakened to a sliver of moon floating in the night sky. I heard the Girls ripping up grasses and munching in rhythmic unison. This time, their presence was comforting. I felt safe with them there. They wouldn't linger if a cougar were anywhere nearby.

Before dawn, I got up, unzipped my tent, and looked out. The Girls were gone. The smell of digested grass and manure wafted from a pile somewhere close. I crawled out and stood under a bowl of glittering stars. I pictured the Girls' great lurking heads peering down through my tent window. Where had they come from? Why had they sought me out and hung around for so long?

I chose my steps carefully back to my tent, avoiding fresh piles, and crawled into my warm bag. I lay there, heavy-hearted and longing for my nighttime companions. I fell back to sleep dreaming of how I might capture that beautiful indigo starry sky with two equine silhouettes in a painting, in gratitude for my preternatural visitors.

RESURRECTING WILDNESS

Nature is full of genius,
full of divinity, full of magic.
—Author unknown

Halfway through the night, a shower of juniper berries and twigs plopped down onto my face and tumbled over the pillow.

"Knock it off!" I yelled into the darkness. I brushed the debris away, rolled onto my side, and pulled the covers up close. This was the second night of my solo fast back in the Modoc National Forest, which had become my favorite questing place. This time my power place was tucked in under the massive lower limbs of a grand old juniper—sheltered and shady. I loved the routine of questing in the Modoc, but aging had brought other predictable routines and habits that had started to feel like the old cliché of wagon ruts in a road. I couldn't remember the last time I'd caught a glimpse of the shimmering moon and imagined my own wild magic.

I was bored with myself. I'd lost my mojo. I wanted to break up the pattern and be in the thick of wild nature.

How could I reignite the wildness in me?

All was quiet. Briefly. Then the shuffling and snapping of twigs started up again. My hollowed-out stomach already had me corkscrewing in my sleeping bag. Add to that the business going on in the tree overhead, and a good night's sleep was impossible. I reached under my pillow and found my flashlight, pulled it out, turned it on, and shined it up into the tree branches. I flinched. Two beady eyes, a pair of translucent ears, and a pink nose appeared in the flashlight beam, no more than four feet from my face. A pack rat.

"Could you please stop dropping stuff on my head?" I asked.

The creature, upright on its back haunches, peered down at me. With its clawed front feet pulled up under its chin, it resembled a miniature begging dog. Its furry white under-belly reflected the light like a surrender flag. I was thinking the rat was cute with its teddy-bear ears and little button eyes. Then I spied something horizontal and shiny between its whiskers. Clenched in its front toothpick-like incisors were my silver feather earrings, my ceremonial earrings, the ones I'd worn on every wilderness quest for the last fifteen years.

I bolted upright. "You little shit!"

The pack rat skittered down the limb, launched itself across the foot of my sleeping bag, and disappeared. Pack rats, also known as wood rats or jumping mice, make a living out of collecting flotsam and jetsam from the forest floor during their nightly forays and hauling it back to their nests. It was bad enough that the critter had stolen my earrings; the rat's boldness to run right over me afterward was downright insulting. When I'd gone to bed that night, I'd placed the earrings under a handkerchief next to my pillow. I should have known better. At least it was only earrings, not something important. I thought back to what had happened to my friend Susanne on a quest two years earlier.

Susanne stood on the road, shading her eyes from the bright morning light. She had a red bandanna tied around her gray hair and wore the same dark pants and light shirt that she'd had on four days earlier when we parted ways for our solo fasting time. She and I, along with the Wild Hearts, had quested in the Modoc again that year. We considered the place ours. When I saw Susanne on the road, I unbuckled my hip belt, dropped my bulky backpack to the ground, and set off to meet her.

"I'm so glad to see you," she said.

We hugged tightly, and her hair smelled of sage. She started to cry. I eased back and looked at her. Something was different about Susanne, but I couldn't figure out what it was.

"What happened?" I asked.

"My glasses," she said, motioning toward her face. "The pack rats."

Now I saw what was different about her. Susanne always wore her glasses, could barely see without them. Her face looked strange and naked. Four days earlier, she had shown me her power place at the base of a two-hundred-foot cliff. Scattered across the flat ground around her site were dozens of gigantic rocks as big as trucks. Fifty feet up the hill was a huge pack rat nest.

"This is my spot," Susanne said, pointing to a flat place between two boulders.

"Holy smokes! That's the biggest pack rat nest I've ever seen," I said, looking uphill. "Your site is really close to it."

"I plan to let the rats go about their business, and hopefully they'll let me go about mine," she'd said. Little did she know that four days later, the rats would have robbed her blind.

Back on the road, I took Susanne's hand. "Those little stinkers," I said.

"I should have known not to leave them out. But I didn't think they would make off with something that heavy. I really need my glasses." Tears welled up in her green eyes.

Susanne and I had quested together every year for six years, shared life stories, and developed a deep kinship. "Come on," I said. "Take my hiking poles. Let's go look for them."

We headed down the road to her spot among the rocks. Morning sun had not yet reached the area, and the boulders held tight to nighttime freezing temperatures. Susanne sat down on a rock and huddled in her sleeping bag. The rat's nest heaped up like a brown igloo wedged between two rocks. Twice my height, it was a twisted menagerie with three visible holes, one near the bottom and two higher up. On my hands and knees, I peered into the first hole cautiously. I imagined a snarling rodent jumping out at me but saw only piles of rat feces, pieces of paper, and mounds of twigs.

"Nothing yet," I yelled.

The other two holes were about eight feet up. Climbing straight up the nest was impossible. It was too precarious, and the whole thing might collapse under my weight. I scrambled up a slanted rock face, held on to a limb, and sidestepped over to the massive twig pile.

"Be careful," Susanne said.

"I'm okay."

I scrunched down under low-hanging branches and crawled my way across the rock that pressed ice-cold against my belly. When I reached the second hole, I peered through a grapefruit-sized door and waited for something to jump out at me. But there were no rats, only an open chamber with all manner of junk poked in—fluorescent orange surveyor tape, feathers, silvery pop-tops, bits of paper, bone fragments, branches, twigs, shriveled berries, and other plant materials. I thought of the millions of trips it took for a pack rat to build up such an impressive mound of debris. It was a fascinating hoard. Backing away, I held on to a juniper limb and crossed over to the third hole. Lying out flat, black rat droppings too close to my nose, I leaned in and looked. There at the threshold, folded up tidy and sparkling, was a pair of silver wire-rimmed glasses.

I gazed up through the silhouetted juniper limbs at a crescent moon and smiled at this memory, at the same time doubting I'd ever see my silver earrings again—wouldn't even know where to start looking. I lay there under the juniper thinking about the pack rat's dark button eyes staring down at me with the flash of silver between its teeth, and my mind drifted to another memory.

It was a dark, cold late-October morning when we headed out for the hunting trip. It was 1970, and I had just turned nineteen. Bob and I had been married for three years, and he had decided we should go deer hunting together. He was an avid hunter, and I was anxious to please him, so I agreed. He was thrilled when we married because this allowed him to shoot one deer for every adult member of his family. No one in my family had ever hunted or owned guns, but we weren't opposed to hunting either. Bob would buy four deer tags from the California Department of Fish and Game—one for him, one for me, and one for each of my parents—and he would hunt and kill four deer himself. We would butcher the animals ourselves, piling up white packages of deer meat in the freezer. By the time our marriage ended seven years later, I was sick to death of venison.

We left before dawn and stopped at a wildlife corridor in the Sierra Nevada Mountains that Bob knew, where herds of deer traveled to and from higher elevations. The recent autumn rain and chilly weather meant the deer were on the move back to lower land for the winter months. Bundled in red-and-black-checked wool jackets and fluorescent orange hunting caps, we parked the truck in front of a closed gate and eased quietly out into the freezing morning. Rifles loaded, we set out on a foot trail with flashlights and hiked up to a rocky outcropping. When daylight came, there would be a full view of the manzanita-covered terrain below.

"Climb up to the highest rock and wait," Bob whispered. "I'll head back down the ridge and flush the deer up your way. If you see a buck that's at least a forked horn, shoot it. Don't shoot a doe, and don't shoot a spike. And for God's sake, don't shoot me."

I smiled and nodded. "Okay," I whispered, then climbed up to a flat granite stone and perched there as instructed. Bob headed back down the trail. Below the rocks, in the murky light, dark brushy mounds stretched out over the terrain, interspersed with barely visible silhouettes of tall conifers. The icy air bit at my cheeks and numbed my hands and feet. Setting the gun aside, I shivered, hugged my body, and jiggled my legs up and down. I wondered how long I'd have to sit there waiting for Bob's return.

At the same time the sun rose over the ridge, a rustling sound erupted from the brush below the rocks. I picked up the gun, pulled one leg up and raised the bolt-action rifle on my knee, then peered through the scope and aimed the crosshairs on the edge of the brush. Branches cracked. I froze in place, barely breathing. A four-point buck high-stepped out of the brambles and into the open. I raised my head from the rifle scope and looked at him. He stood broadside, his full body in view, the perfect position for a good shot. The deer was spectacular and regal looking, with a coat of thick sable-brown hair, a white tail and underbelly, and a bib-shaped swath of white hair on his upper chest. There was a perfect symmetry to his horns, his ears, and the white markings that ran up his snout and across his forehead like an enigmatic crest. Bony antlers curved in a bowl shape high above his head, as if holding space for an invisible crown. My pulse raced. An adrenaline-induced exhilaration washed over my body. Bob had taken me out target shooting several times before hunting season and taught me how to shoot a deer: aim a little higher to account for the force of gravity that would pull the bullet down as it traveled through the air, brace myself for the kickback of the stock, then squeeze the trigger. His voice echoed: *Don't shoot it in the gut. Aim just above and a little behind the front leg to hit the heart and lungs.* I pressed the gun stock against my shoulder and set the crosshairs above the front left leg. The buck caught my scent, turned his head, and faced me dead-on. The hair rose on the back of my neck. Long black lashes framed the buck's eyes, and a glint of light reflected off his black pupils.

We stayed eye to eye for several seconds—plenty of time to send a bullet through his heart. I felt something pass between us. I lowered the rifle. "Run!" I yelled, my voice piercing the quiet morning and ricocheting around the brushy terrain. The buck leaped up and ran down over the hill. I took in a deep breath and let it go with a sigh. A half hour later Bob came hiking up the trail.

"Did you see any deer?"

I gazed out over the manzanita field where the buck had disappeared. "No," I said. I felt Bob's eyes linger on me, but I didn't look back at him. It was one of many differences between us. Whereas Bob saw nature as something to conquer, for me, that day was the first time I experienced the sacred connection of being eye to eye with something wild, majestic, and extraordinary that should never be destroyed.

On the next night of my wilderness quest, it wasn't pack rats or memories of deer hunting that kept me awake, but coyotes—a whole pack of them yipping and howling and carrying on out on the plain. Deer are plentiful in the Modoc, and I wondered if the pack was celebrating a kill. I rolled onto my back and calculated the distance between where I lay and the barking screams. No more than a quarter of a mile, I figured. The cries were unsettling, not because I feared the coyotes would come and eat me—I'd never heard of coyotes attacking people. It was more like something in my primal brain was blasting an alert: *Danger, predators afoot!* I curled onto my side and pulled the cover over my head. Eventually the coyotes quieted down, and I finally drifted off to sleep.

The next morning, I set out on my usual walkabout, through needle-leaved sagebrush and juniper trees. It was a calm sunny morning, and the meadowlarks trilled as if happy for another day. Red-tailed hawks soared in necklace-like dips across the cloudless blue sky. I wandered out on my foray, scanning the ground in search of wild remnants: feathers, bones, or unique rocks to collect. I smiled to myself at the irony of how my behavior resembled that of the pack rat. I had been so annoyed with the little scavenger the night before, and here I was mimicking it. Both of us hunting for treasures. Both of us responding to a wild instinct to seek out, find, and take for our own.

Following game trails that wove through the meadow grass and around brushy mounds, I crossed fresh coyote scat—lots of it. Palm-sized, crisscrossed piles of dark cigar-shaped poop filled with fur, berries, and small bones, deposited right in the middle of the trail like a calling card: *Coyote was here.* I continued to walk the narrow animal trail that faded in and out of view, so faint in places I struggled to follow it. I'd pick it up again by the telltale clues of broken stems, upturned leaves, or crushed grasses. I didn't know how or when I'd learned to follow a trail like that; it seemed to come naturally.

At the bottom of an incline, a short distance ahead, I spotted a dark rectangular shape. At best, it appeared to be a tree stump, but was too thin and squared off. Then I realized it was a rotting fence post, evidently left over from mid-twentieth-century cattle ranching in the area. A tangle of rusty barbed wire hung from the post. The other end of the wire snaked across the trail and flattened into the humus. Atop the flat barbed section of wire lay another pile of speckled coyote scat.

Two years earlier, I'd been traveling with my friend Jim along a highway outside of Taos, New Mexico, and caught a glimpse of something out the passenger-side window. "Stop!" I yelled. "Turn around. Go back. There's something I want to see."

"What is it?" he asked, easing back on the gas, the car slowing. Jim, ten years older than I and in good physical shape, did most of the driving on our annual hiking adventures. I was grateful for the chance to sit back and take in all the scenery.

"I'm not sure . . . but it's worth turning around. I promise."

Jim circled around and drove back to a fence line along the east side of the two-lane road. The car stopped. I got out and sidestepped my way down into a five-foot ditch, up the other side, and through knee-high brush for a closer look. I heard Jim get out and follow behind me. The body shape-shifted, first into a deer, then into a wolf, then into itself. Coyote. He was big for his breed, thick-furred and healthy looking. There he hung, folded in two, his back haunch draped over one side of the barbed wire, the rest of his body—gut, chest, and head—folded down over the other side, hanging free, his nose six inches from the ground, tongue lopped over his lower lip in a caricature death scene. I bent down and looked into his golden-brown eyes. I saw only a lifeless, blank stare. It was quiet carnage with no sign of a struggle. A bloody pool beneath his nose had soaked into the dirt and left a red oxide stain. Dried crimson splotches dotted over yellow blooms of rabbit brush. His lush fur lay in rich waves of color over his back and down onto his tail, paws clean, black toe pads round and plump. It was like a taxidermy scene replicated to illustrate the dangerous life of a coyote.

I reached out and touched him. I felt like I was touching something sacred, but it also felt blasphemous, like reaching for something holy and wild that shouldn't be disturbed. My finger met with furry rigor. Solid. He had been dead for a while. No bullet holes, no sign of any struggle. He was just hanging there, lifeless. I imagined how it had gone. At dusk he had left his den and trotted along through bristled thicket, stirring up sage, nose hovering low, picking up scent. He had not eaten for days. On the other side of the ravine, he caught sight of the hare. He crouched down and eased in for the kill. In a burst of dust, the rabbit leaped up, shot across the dirt, and zigzagged through the sagebrush. The coyote launched into full pursuit, and the chase was on, first north through the thick sage, then west toward the highway. He'd seen the fence at the last minute, made a leap to clear it, but the barbed wire had done its job, and he was caught at the hip—the underside of vital organs, the back of his long strong body snapped to a stop, hind legs pawing with no purchase to free himself. The more he struggled, the deeper the wire pierced his tender parts. He must have died quickly, his spine snapping in two from trajectory force.

"Ready to get going?" Jim asked.

I jumped at the sound of his voice. I'd forgotten he was behind me. "No, wait a second," I said. "I want to check him out some more."

"It's a dead coyote, GG," he said, "There's nothing you can do."

"No, it's more than that. I don't know . . ."

Jim started walking back to the car, but I couldn't turn away. I inspected the hairy fur, light tawny brown with deep brown tips. Behind the ears and over the forelegs, the color changed to the red brown of the New Mexico landscape. The underside of his body was creamy white, the tip of the tail carbon black, all designed for camouflage to disappear into the variegated terrain. It was the paws that got to me. One crossed over the other in a peaceful gesture, anthropo-morphic in a dead man's pose. For a moment I wanted to cut off his tail, turn it into artwork as a keepsake of the find, but I couldn't bring myself to disturb the beauty. He was too perfect, so Christlike in his hip belt of thorns. Christ on the cross. Coyote on the fence.

This was his territory to run free and mark with scat on downed barbed wire fences. How could he have known a landowner had set a trap to thwart his rabbit chase, a barrier barely visible in the dim evening light? Doing what comes naturally, he got caught in a gut snare. The whole scene was horrific, tragic, captivating, and exhilarating—exquisite wildness stopped in midstride and hung up on the fence to

die. It felt good to revere something, love something, hurt for
it. It was the same love and hurt I felt for my own wild spirit.
My life had become tame and conventional, so predictable.
Was my wildness dying too?

Over the next few nights, the coyote came to me in my
dreams three times. In the first dream, I floated toward him,
my feet not touching the ground. I poked at him, and he
came to life, finished his jump over the fence, and ran away
free. It felt exhilarating. In the second, I stood perplexed in
front of a painting of a dead coyote on the fence that hung
at an art gallery, wondering how someone had painted the
exact same scene. In the third, I stood at the fence, and this
time he turned his head, eyes riveted on me, and spoke in a
low, haunting whisper: "Do you get it?"

Weeks later, back home in Oregon after the New Mexico
vacation, the memory of the coyote had stayed with me.
I sat in a dining room chair at breakfast, closed my eyes,
and felt emotions rise like an ocean wave. I wanted to shake
things up and coax the animal inside me out into the meadow
before it got sacrificed in a barbed wire trap of conventional
limitation. The summer before, I could have worn feathers
in my hair and joined ecstatic dance in the drum tower at
the Oregon Country Fair. The rhythm filled my body, but I
held back, reined it in, afraid I'd look like a silly old woman,
afraid I would embarrass my kids, myself. Could have. But
didn't. Once, while painting on a giant canvas in an art class,
I wanted to take off my clothes, cover my body in paint, then
lie down and roll around on the canvas. I could have been that
eccentric old lady who stripped down and used her body as a
paintbrush in art class. Could have. But wasn't.

Back in the Modoc on the trail to my campsite, I stepped over the pile of coyote scat, choosing my footing carefully to avoid the barbed wire. I traveled through the grassy meadow to my place under the sprawling juniper. I stretched out in the shade and looked up at windows of open sky between the crisscrossed branches of the brushy conifer and sifted through the memories of the pack rats, the deer, and the coyote. The flashback of the search for Susanne's glasses made me smile. The deer-hunting memory made my head shake back and forth in a definitive no. But the recollection of the coyote on the fence was visceral.

At sunrise I packed up my gear and headed back to base camp. On the way, I stopped at a clump of sagebrush, pulled off a handful of leaves, brought them to my nose, and breathed in. The aroma sent a sharp cooling sensation through my body, and I wanted to go back to the moment I had seen that coyote, stroked its thick fur, and felt wildness against my fingertips. Questing had renewed and reinvigorated the wildness in me. I had sunbathed nude in Death Valley, danced naked in a thunderstorm in the Inyo Mountains, and put mud on my face and sticks and lichens in my hair and held a ceremonial funeral for dead reptiles—all exhilarating experiences. Coyote beckoned me to leap out into the unknown and let wildness have its way with me once more. I wanted to crawl into coyote's empty pelt, come back to life, and feel my four feet fly out across the chaparral.

On a warm August day a few months after my quest, I went down to my local art store and purchased a giant roll of canvas and six jars of tempera paint: blue, green, red, yellow, purple, and orange. I invited two artist friends to my studio, spread the canvas out on the floor, wall to wall. I opened the paints and placed a fat brush in each jar, then we slipped off our clothes and started in.

SEARCHING
FOR COYOTE

*If you want others to be happy, practice compassion. If
you want yourself to be happy, practice compassion.*
—The Dalai Lama

Conifers swayed in the morning breeze, a sound somewhere between a whisper and a whoosh. A fledgling
hawk flew overhead with a screeching *kree-ah*, *kree-ah* and
landed, camouflaged in the dark woods. My quest was in
the most resplendent place I'd ever been, the Inyo National
Forest in Central California. My power place was at the foot
of obsidian-covered Glass Mountain, in a forest of pine and
mahogany trees, and at the edge of a meadow alive with wildflowers. Knowing the Inyo was considered the dwelling place
of the Great Spirit, my intention for my wilderness quest that
year was to call upon the wisdom of that spirit as I journeyed
deeper into understanding my relationship with my father
and making peace with my past.

How might signs from nature help me heal the wounds that led me to mistrust men?

I rested in my camp chair at the meadow's edge and savored the bucolic scene of two deer standing in the clearing, munching new grass. Suddenly, the deer raised their heads, leaped up, and dashed into the forest. At the edge of the trees stood a tan-and-gray, four-footed animal with a long muzzle and perked-up ears. A dog? No. Coyote, a powerful messenger for me. The coyote lowered its head and prowled out into the meadow. I lifted my binoculars and sighted on the animal as it picked up pace and disappeared behind a bush. I waited but never saw the coyote emerge from the bramble. Keeping one eye on the meadow, I tugged on my boots, grabbed my day pack and hiking poles, and headed toward the place where the coyote had disappeared. I wanted a closer look, curious about where the beast had gone. I pushed through waist-high meadow grass and over lumpy terrain that turned my feet and pulled at my ankles. I came to the tangled mass of foliage where I had last spied the coyote and peered in. Nothing. No coyote, no hole. Only brush and dry cracked mud.

Native legends tell of the enigmatic coyote—playful and wise, trickster and teacher. Here one moment, gone the next. Coyote had vanished into thin air. What trick was he playing? What was he here to teach? When I was a kid, my father and I watched Saturday morning cartoons. He laughed uproariously at Wile E. Coyote and the elusive Road Runner. My father's easy, boisterous laugh was contagious, and soon I was laughing too. When sober, my father was witty, clever, and fun to be around. His well-proportioned face had a straight nose, strong cheekbones, and a wide affable smile. His eyes sparkled with life. He was always sober and especially happy when he took us camping. On one of our trips, he made a portable medicine cabinet with a mirror that he hung from a tree limb. He whittled long sticks for marshmallow roasting and stacked wood in a neat pile next to the firepit. He took us on long hikes and entertained everyone with songs and silly jokes. Those happy moments with my father made the times he disappeared into the sinkhole of the bottle more painful.

My father would stop drinking for years at a time, long enough for us to think it was all over. But we didn't understand the disease of alcoholism, how it hijacks the brain and dissolves willpower like candle wax in a hot flame. It was only a matter of time before he picked up another drink and the whole cycle began again, sabotaging any hope for his talents and gifts to be fully expressed in the world.

Milo Benjamin Derkum was what they called a *body and fender man*, back when cars were made of chrome, metal, and steel. His work was impeccable, and he was sought after by all the best auto body repair shops in town. He could make a wrecked car look new through a meticulous process of applying lead with a blowtorch, sanding out the imperfections, then spray-painting the surface. The result was a car body good as new. But the process left my father's body wrecked with emphysema.

On my eighth birthday, during one of his longer sober spells, my father made me a set of handcrafted wooden doll furniture. I was thrilled with the Barbie-sized couch and chair with slanted wood backs and small armrests attached with finishing nails. He had stained the furniture walnut brown, and the couch and chair seats were the exact length of Barbie's legs from hip to knee. My father must have measured carefully to get everything to fit exactly right. When he wasn't drinking,

I would feel safe and playful again, instead of the watchful child of an alcoholic, and would spend hours arranging and rearranging Barbie and Ken's living room furniture on the patio of our suburban home. A white doily served as a living room rug. My mother had sewn Polynesian print cushions for the wooden couch and chair. I picked tiny pink phlox flowers from the garden and poked them into a miniature cone-shaped aluminum foil vase. I was pleased with how perfect my bouquet looked on the coffee table, along with a Barbie-sized ceramic tea set.

One day, though, as I played with my dolls and arranged their furniture, my father's voice boomed out from the bedroom window a few yards from where I was playing. His words slurred as he belted out an old song: "You'll never know just how much I love you. You'll never know just how much I care." I froze, Barbie in one hand, Ken in the other, a surge of dread in my gut. I abandoned the dolls, tiptoed over, and looked through the window at my father sitting on the edge of the bed in his boxer shorts. His thick, wavy salt-and-pepper hair, which he wore combed straight back, fell disheveled over his face. He leaned forward, palms together, a cigarette between the two tobacco-stained fingers of his right hand. It was his drinking position. Memories of past binges roiled in my stomach—the fighting and yelling, the household upheaval, and the feeling of helplessness that pulled me down into a sad, dark hole. This binge, like all the others, would end up in one of two ways: he either passed out cold and woke up the next morning sick and retching, or he kept drinking and smoking all night and insisted on driving himself to work. Either scenario inevitably concluded with another job loss and a cold silence that wintered over the house for days.

My father died when I was sixteen. By the time I went on my wilderness quest in the Inyo, he had been gone for fifty years. I still missed him. He would have followed the coyote in the meadow too.

With coyote nowhere to be found, I picked my way through the slog and moved deeper into the field. Out toward the middle, where the grasses gleamed an emerald green, the surface turned to swampy sponge-moss and oozed up around my ankle-high boots. I searched for drier footfalls, but my next steps met bottomlessness. Without warning, my feet sank straight down into a thick, muddy crevasse, and I was hanging free in the dirty goop. I hung there, upright in the hole with no ground beneath my feet, submerged from the waist down. *Quicksand? How deep would I go?* My bulky day pack was all that had stopped me from falling farther in. "Holy shit!" I sucked in deep, short gasps and railed my legs against the narrow slit. The cold mud pressed in against my skin, and I was trapped.

My adrenaline kicked in, and with hiking poles still in my hands, I dug one tip into the semisolid ground and tried to pull myself up. But the narrow fissure prevented any bend in my knees. I pushed my feet against the muddy sides, but each attempt at leverage dissolved into squishy nothingness. *Stop thrashing around and think.* I tossed aside my hiking poles, pressed both hands into the boggy ground, and pushed. After a few tries, I took a deep breath, gave it all I had, and heaved myself up and out, landing face-first in the grass. The impact hurt my nose and mouth, but the solid ground beneath me was a welcome relief. Rolling over onto my back, I held my burning nose for a moment. I looked down at two gooey, lead-colored appendages barely recognizable as my own.

The ravine across the street from where I had grown up had that same oozy gray clay after it rained, and that muddy gulch offered me refuge one autumn day around my ninth birthday. I'd been playing baseball in the yard with the neighbor kids and came charging through the front door for a snack. My mother sat on the edge of a chair, her lips pursed, legs crossed at the ankles. My father sat on the couch, his face white and weary, his blue eyes watery and sad. A green plaid shirt that once fit his muscular body now fell loosely over his fragile rib cage. He leaned forward, elbows resting on widespread knees, hands clasped together. A stranger in a dark suit sat next to him, mirroring my father's posture.

"This is Mr. Smith," my mother said. "He's going to help your dad stop drinking." She normally spoke about my father's drinking in vague terms like "the situation with your dad" or "it's not a good day to have any friends over." The directness was new.

The man smiled at me. He had a brown crew cut and wore shiny shoes with socks that matched his navy suit. "Your dad will be going with me to meetings," he said. "There will be other people there who are trying to stop drinking too."

My father looked up at me, offered a tight-lipped smile, then glanced down at his shoes.

"Oh . . . okay," I said. Would it really work this time? My father had stopped drinking before. During those times, in the evenings after my bath, I'd put on my flannel pajamas and sit next to him while we watched television shows like *Father Knows Best* and *Mr. Ed, the Talking Horse*. But those times were short-lived, and he eventually fell back into the bottle.

Forgetting the snack, I pivoted and slipped out the door. Instead of going back to the baseball game, I crossed the road to a well-worn path through the tall grass and down into the ravine. At the creek's edge, I squatted down in the mud and peered into the water at globs of green gelatinous frog eggs floating on the surface. In the middle of the pool, tadpoles darkened the sandy creek bed, a legion of miniature brown balloons on wiggly strings. I cupped my hands together and dipped into the water. Two tadpoles swam into my palms, tails undulating back and forth. Their tiny dark bodies nudged against my hand searching for a way out. One was a half tadpole, half frog, with sprouted back legs. I lowered my hands back into the water, and the less developed one swam out and sank to the creek bottom. When I pulled my hands back, the half frog, half tadpole, having been stuck in a finger crease, flew out and flopped around in the mud.

Panicked, I tried to pick it up, but it was like trying to get a grip on an oiled pea. In the mud by the creek lay a wide green leaf. I slipped it under the tadpole and gently rolled the little round creature to the center crease. I folded the leaf and submerged the bundle into the creek. The almost-frog kicked wildly into the leafy debris and disappeared into the creek bottom. "You're safe, little pollywog," I said.

After my parents divorced, I visited my father for an overnight stay on my twelfth birthday. He sat in his small apartment in an easy chair marked with a dark stain where his head rubbed the back. A butt-filled ashtray and a glass half-full of Old Crow whiskey sat on a small table beside him. I curled up on a dingy green couch pocked with burn holes and held one arm around Scruffy, my father's little brown-and-white dog. My father leaned forward in a cloud of cigarette smoke with his elbows pinned to his knees and stared at the floor. "Your mother is a bitch and a whore," he said. His words slid out loose and slurred. I knew what a whore was, and my face caught fire. I said nothing, pulled my knees to my chest, and glared sideways at my father through a watery curtain of tears. I wanted to call my mom and go home, but she was out for the evening.

My father continued to rant about my mother between gulps of whiskey and drags on cigarettes. When it was time for bed, I unrolled my sleeping bag and retreated into a small alcove at the end of the hallway between two closed doors, in front of a full-length mirror. I tucked Scruffy under one arm, cuddled his warm, wiry-haired body close, and stared at our dark reflections in the mirror until I fell asleep. That was the last time I visited my father. My mother picked me up early the next day, and a few years later, my father died of heart failure. The property owner heard Scruffy barking incessantly day and night, and when she entered the apartment, she found him lying on the bedroom floor. I don't remember much about his funeral, only that I wore a black-and-white houndstooth-patterned dress—and that I didn't cry.

———————

After I pulled out of the crevasse, I steadied myself and then *squish-squished* back to camp. By the time I returned, the putty-colored clay covering my hips and legs had nearly dried. I stripped down to my underwear and hung my shorts, shirt, and socks on a tree limb, then set my boots in the sun. I broke off the hardened chunks of gray mud from my skin, poured water onto a hanky, and wiped my legs and arms. Cleaned up and dressed, I felt a calling to go back out into the meadow and find the place where I had fallen into the crevasse. The wild child in me wanted to jump back in the hole and cover my whole body with mud, like pictures of Aboriginal people I'd seen in *National Geographic*. But there was something else too. That dark, scary hole reminded me of the bottomless pit I fell into every time my father picked up the bottle.

With a pocketful of obsidian chips, I followed my muddy footprints back to the hole. I stood over the mucky fissure and, one by one, dropped pieces of sharp, shiny obsidian into the hole. With each chip I released, I imagined letting go of repressed anger and resentment toward my father. I wondered if I had known my dad when I was an adult, would we have had things in common? An aunt once told me he was smart, clever, witty, and talented. I missed the man I never really knew. I would never have a chance to know my father better, but I could remember the good things I loved about him and find it in my heart to forgive him.

Suddenly, the elusive coyote appeared again, out of nowhere, trotting along at the far edge of the meadow, heading straight toward me. He broke into a graceful run, loping through the tall dry grass, moving closer and closer. At the last minute, before I could make out the color of his eyes, he turned and dissolved into the dark forest. Coyote came only so close, then disappeared into a shadowy refuge. Just like my dad.

BREAKING
AND MENDING

The wound is the place where the light enters you.
—Rumi

A ray of morning sunlight filtered through the pines and shined a spotlight on an indigo-blue ceramic bowl sitting on a tree stump. I pulled my camp chair closer to the stump and waited until I felt ready. I turned the bowl upside down and draped a red handkerchief over it. Then I picked up a fist-sized obsidian rock, raised my arm, and came down hard. The obsidian met the vessel with a *clunk*. At the same time the bowl shattered, a hawk flew out of the forest. I watched the hawk curve through the ocean-blue sky and soar around and around in tight circles above me.

I pressed my hands over the handkerchief and let the broken pieces of the bowl jab into my palms. I lifted the edge of the handkerchief and peeked in. Deep blue shards of pottery lay scattered like broken shells on a beach. I turned each piece right side up and arranged them back into a circular shape. How would all these broken pieces fit back together and make the vessel whole again?

Breaking the bowl on my wilderness quest was a symbolic entry into the West shield of the Medicine Wheel, the territory of reflection and introspection. Again, I wanted to make peace with my past, this time using the ceremony of breaking and mending to reconcile an unresolved relationship with my brother, Mickey. Mickey had been mean to me when we were kids, and I still felt anger and resentment about it. I never had the courage to tell him how I felt before he died eight years earlier. Recently I'd had a dream in which he stood in front of me and leaned forward as if to say something. I waited for him to speak, but nothing came.

The dream felt like an omen. I wanted to clean up unresolved issues with my family and age gracefully without lingering resentment. I had watched my father sink into anger and bitterness in his final years. I had sat beside my ninety-nine-year-old mother and listened to her drift into longings and regrets. I didn't want to grow old like that; I wanted to resolve my conflicted feelings about Mickey.

Was it possible to find love and compassion for my brother even after he was gone?

I had planned to break the bowl the day before but had stopped myself. I wasn't ready; it felt too violent. There was no hurry. I had put the bowl on a flat tree stump, left it sitting in the open, and walked over to the edge of the forest where the acres-long meadow stretched out green and gold in the morning sun. The aspens quiver-shook shimmering glints of yellow against an eternal blue sky. Swarms of flying insects glistened like daytime stars over the dewy grass. A squawking cry from another hawk pierced my solitude, and I searched the green boughs of a nearby towering Jeffrey pine but couldn't find its hiding place.

Mickey could imitate a hawk's cry that sounded like the real thing: a high-pitched whistle that dipped and faded off. *Kee-eeeee-arr.* I pictured the art he painted, floor to ceiling, on the walls of his bedroom—giant Salvador Dalí-ish melting faces and body parts. I used to sneak my friends into his room when he wasn't home and show them the fascinating and disturbing images. Mickey could create anything: illustrations, paintings, ceramics, and cool forts in the tree-lined ravine across the street from the house where we grew up. I sat next to him at the kitchen table, his thick dark hair cascading over his forehead as he hunched over his paper doodling the image of Alfred E. Neuman from *Mad Magazine.* I was amazed by his ability to sketch exact facial details from memory. He printed a row of letters evenly beneath the image: *What, me worry?* But Mickey didn't like me watching him draw. "Get lost," he'd bark, and I'd slink away, brokenhearted.

My wilderness bowl-breaking ceremony was called *kintsugi* in Japanese, which translates as "golden joinery." *Kintsugi* is a breaking and mending ritual in which you intentionally break an object, glue it back together, and paint the cracks with gold. The philosophy is based on the idea of embracing imperfection. It highlights cracks and repairs as natural events in the life of a bowl or cup, rather than allowing its service to end when it gets damaged or broken. I had been bringing people together in my art studio for "Kintsugi Breaking and Mending" ceremonies over the past year. Now, I wanted to experience the ritual for personal reasons.

The day before I broke the bowl, a hawk had flown out of the dark woods and soared over my campsite. Mickey would have loved to be there in the company of hawks. The raptors would have been his totem animal if he'd believed that humans have a mystical relationship with animals. Maybe he did; I'd never know. What I did know was that the presence of the hawks felt like an invitation to break and mend the *kintsugi* bowl in memory of my brother. I covered the bowl with a handkerchief, picked up an apple-sized chunk of coal-black obsidian, raised it over the bowl, and tapped it on the surface to test the weight. But instead of following through with the bowl breaking that day, I set the rock down on the stump and followed the scene that had begun to replay in my head.

I was thirteen years old, standing in our mint-green-tiled bathroom getting ready for school. It was seventh-grade picture day. I'd chosen my outfit the night before, a magenta pleated skirt and matching plaid blouse, and I'd slept on brush rollers—painful but effective. Standing in front of the mirror, I backcombed my hair, smoothed it down, and picked up a can of Aquanet. I held my breath and sprayed a sticky cloud around my head, then clipped a pink bow in the flat space between my straight bangs and the brown mound of helmet-shaped hair. I pressed my hand along the sides, checked for stiffness, then sprayed the bouffant again.

My mother had divorced my father a year earlier. She worked long hours during the day teaching school and was out most evenings, enjoying her new life as a single woman. This left me home alone with Mickey, who was seventeen years old at the time. A crash reverberated from the front part of the house. I set the hairspray on the counter and hurried down the hall to the kitchen. Shattered dishes, silverware, food, and dirt were strewn across the blue linoleum floor. The table and chairs were overturned. Pieces of a broken planter and green stems lay in a puddle of coffee.

"Mickey!" I screamed. "Mickey!"

My brother twitched and jerked. His rigid body jolted

up and down on the floor like a fish in a hot frying pan. White foam oozed from his grimaced lips. Frantic, I dashed out the front door, through the yard, and up the path of the house next door. I raced up the steps and banged on the screen. Sherry opened the door and stood with a half-eaten slice of toast in her hand. She had been my playmate since we'd moved to the California suburb in the mid-fifties.

"There's something wrong with my brother," I said, my voice high in a panic. "Is your dad home? He needs to come over and help."

Warren appeared at the front door in a white T-shirt and striped boxer shorts, his hair disheveled. "What's wrong?" he asked.

"My brother is lying on the floor and jerking all around."

Warren maneuvered around Sherry and me, letting the screen door slam behind him. He dashed down the stairs and across the lawn to our open front door. I followed, terrified. When I got to our kitchen, Warren was on the floor, leaning over my brother and holding his head. He tried to shove a wad of paper napkins into my brother's mouth, but Mickey's teeth were clenched tight. Tossing the wad aside, Warren grasped Mickey's arms and held his shoulders down while his body thrashed. I stood back and watched with tears streaming down my face. Then, as if a switch had flipped, Mickey stopped. I took it all in—my brother on the floor, Warren in his underwear, the eggs, toast, coffee, overturned kitchen table, and silence.

"Mike," Warren said, breaking the eerie quiet. "Mike, are you okay? Can you hear me?"

Mickey fluttered his eyes and took in a deep breath. "What . . . what happened?" he asked. He pulled up onto his elbows and looked around, then over at me. "What the hell happened?"

"I think you had a seizure or something, Mike," Warren said, sitting back on his heels.

Mickey blinked, stared straight ahead, then dropped back down. "I'm just really tired," he said.

Warren stood up and settled his boxer shorts on his waist. "You'll be okay," he said. "Let's get you into bed."

Together, we managed to get Mickey up and onto his feet. A wide dark blotch stained the front of his jeans. I spotted it, wide-eyed.

Mickey caught me staring. "Get the hell out of here!" he yelled.

I backed away and slipped around the corner into the living room, out of sight. Warren guided my brother down the hall to his bedroom. When he returned to the kitchen, we cleaned up the mess together. I picked up the shattered dishes and threw them into the garbage. Warren set the kitchen table back up and placed the four chairs around the sides. He found the mop and cleaned the floor.

"Does your brother have epilepsy?" he asked.

"I don't know; I don't think so."

"I'll call your mom and tell her what happened. You go ahead and go to school."

I retreated to my bedroom, sat down on my bed, and stared at the wall. What had happened to my brother? What would happen to him now?

On the stump next to me, my *kintsugi* bowl glistened in the sun like a Fabergé egg, unspoiled and whole, the way our family might have been without all the trauma caused by alcoholism. *Tomorrow. I'll break the bowl tomorrow.*

Antsy and wanting to move, I wandered out into the meadow and ambled through knee-high tasseled grasses that swished over my bare legs. A black-and-gold monarch butterfly wafted by, landed on a white yarrow flower, and worked its hairlike proboscis over the blossom. I wondered how a creature so fragile-looking withstood a thousand-mile migration: one wingbeat at a time. Again, a hawk cried out from a nearby tree. I meandered through the meadow, and the memory of my brother's epileptic seizure picked up where it had left off. That evening, my mother stood at the stove cooking dinner. I sat at the kitchen table watching Mickey's every move. He had come out of his room, made a peanut butter sandwich, and poured a glass of milk. His thick dark hair was smashed down in places and stood straight up in others from lying in bed all day. He glared at me. "Stop staring at me," he snapped.

I averted my stare to the floor, but then it came back up. Maybe I was afraid, or maybe I was trying to make sure he was still the same person. Whatever the reason, I couldn't keep my eyes off him. The staring sent him into a rage. My brother hauled off and slapped me on the side of the head. The blow knocked me off the chair and onto the floor. I lay in a fetal position, my head buried in my arms. A dull thud surged through my brain, followed by an excruciating ache, followed by a crush of sobs.

"Mike," my mom yelled. "For heaven's sake, the seizure wasn't her fault!" And that was the last time my brother's epilepsy was ever mentioned in our family.

I meandered through the mountain meadow all that afternoon with the grasses, wildflowers, and deer, relishing the quiet and steeped in memories of my brother—his Johnny Cash records, the way he held a cigarette between his thumb and forefinger, and the time he caught his wife sleeping with another man and stabbed him in the gut. "It felt like slicing through butter," he said. He never went to prison for the crime. I'm not sure why. At the end of the day, I readied myself for bed and left the *kintsugi* bowl on its wooden pedestal like an offering, a symbol of my open willingness. In the moonlight, the silhouette of the bowl on the stump presented like a chalice on a dark altar.

———————

After my brother struck me, I kept my distance from him, but I wanted a closer relationship. Mickey grew up to become a brilliant artist, sensitive and funny. He was also an alcoholic, moody, and unavailable, both physically and emotionally. We lived in different states but wrote to one another, shared favorite movies and music. He joined the family for holidays. He called me "Lil' Sis" and I called him "Big Brother." He and I were on our way to repairing our relationship when he died unexpectedly of a stroke in 2007.

The day I finally got the nerve to break the bowl, I lingered with the broken pieces and memories of my brother all that afternoon and the next day. I reconstructed Mickey's life, how things were for him, how things were between us. I closed my eyes and pictured his graduation photo, dressed in a white tux, dark eyes, high cheekbones, full lips, and thick hair slicked back on the sides with a waterfall curl, like Elvis Presley's, tumbling over his forehead. I wished I had just once told him that I loved him.

Late in the afternoon on the final day of my quest, the time felt right to glue the bowl back together, piece by piece, twelve in all. By the time I finished, the sun had moved behind the big Jeffrey pine, casting a shadow over where I worked. I moved my chair out into the warm, bright sun and meticulously painted each crack with gold, brushing the paint along the fault lines and filling in the deeper crevices. One for each of the "get losts," one for the seizure, one for the slap, and one for the *I love you* that I never said. I turned the bowl over and painted the cracks along the underside. When I finished, my *kintsugi* bowl gleamed with zigzagging, lightning-bolt gold lines across the cobalt-blue glaze. I had done it. The bowl was whole again.

I couldn't finish mending my relationship with my brother while he was alive. As a child, I never understood why he had rejected me when we were kids. My memories were fragments of our relationship that I gathered up and glued back together, a symbol of forgiveness of my brother, and myself.

My brother, the only male child in our family, was the one who suffered the most from my father's alcoholism. Like my dad, Mickey didn't know how to navigate the world as a talented, sensitive, complicated man, and there was no one around to show him. Alcoholism took both my father and my brother in their early sixties, young by today's average life expectancy.

I keep a black-and-white photo of my brother and my dad on my dresser, standing together, my brother around eight years old, with my father's arm around his shoulder. Both have the same wide-open smile. They look happy.

Stepping Into
A River of Grief

Grief and love are sisters,
woven together from the beginning.
—Francis Weller

There are times in my life when I get an intuitive feeling that something is right for me, even though on the surface it appears risky and irrational. I wasn't looking for a recreational drug high when I took the ayahuasca journey. It was more like going on another vision quest, this time into the plant medicine realm. I was being called out of my comfort zone into a new level of seeing and understanding beyond the limits of my psyche. I knew somewhere deep down inside that I had to try it.

Ayahuasca, a brewed tea made from the leaves of the *Psychotria viridis* shrub and the *Banisteriopsis caapi* vines that grow in South America, is a powerful psychedelic drink that has been used for centuries by Amazonian tribes in spiritual and religious ceremonies. The person who had served it to me was a bald, middle-aged man with horned-rimmed glasses, sitting cross-legged in the corner of the room, playing a slow melodic tune on a twelve-string guitar. He wore black sweatpants and a black turtleneck shirt. Nearly invisible in the dark, he was illuminated by flickering candlelight that reflected off his shiny forehead, creating the illusion of a flaming third eye. He called himself a *server*, but I thought of him as a shaman, a *curandero*, a traditional Native healer. His job was to serve the brew and lead the ceremony.

Behind this bespectacled *curandero*, more candles shed light on an altar bearing a collection of sacred items: a shell with a stub of palo santo wood that released a stream of gray incense into the air, a large amethyst crystal, an owl wing, and statues of Buddha and Kwan Yin. In the other corner of the room, three assistants, two women and a man, stood ready. It was their job to assist everyone in their journeys with "Grandmother Ayahuasca," as the shaman called it.

Ten journeyers lay on the basement floor of the extravagant three-story home at the edge of a Pacific Northwest forest, with our heads at the wall and our feet toward the center. On the floor by our feet, a three-inch strip of tape glowed an eerie yellowish green. The tape helped the assistants find us in the dark. As I lay on my back, my stomach tingled from the dose of ayahuasca I'd received forty-five minutes earlier.

One of the assistants, a young woman with a silky white sarong draped over her head and body, stood with her hands in prayer pose. She sang a traditional *icaro* song in Quechua, an Indigenous Peruvian language. Sounds rolled off her tongue and floated from her lips like a winged prayer. I surrendered into the hallucination and let myself be carried away with gold and silver threads of music drifting and swirling above me, blissfully unaware of what would unfold over the next several hours.

I had read about ayahuasca years earlier. At first it sounded strange and frightening, and I wanted nothing to do with it. But ayahuasca kept coming back into my life through books and magazine articles. I heard testimonials from friends who'd had life-changing experiences of mind expansion and spiritual breakthroughs after taking DMT (dimethyltryptamine), the chemical element in ayahuasca referred to as "the God molecule."

My curiosity and desire for a personal artistic break-through led me on a search for an ayahuasca guide. I hoped an ayahuasca experience would unleash a whole new level of creative expression in my art and writing. I later learned that, like wilderness questing, ayahuasca brings you what you need—not necessarily what you think you want.

Finding an ayahuasca guide turned out to be more complicated than finding a wilderness-questing guide. Finding a wilderness guide was as simple as picking up a flyer at a bookstore. It took a year and a half for me to find someone experienced and trustworthy for my journey (it's all networking and word-of-mouth), and six more months to get to the top of the waiting list. I had two preliminary interviews, completed a health questionnaire, and fasted for eight hours. And there I was in a strange place on a September night in 2019, stretched out flat on a mattress after having taken a shot glass half-full of the strongest, bitterest muddy-brown guck I'd ever seen, much less ingested.

The angel in white finished crooning her *icaro* melody, then dropped to her knees and onto the floor in a gesture of supplication. She turned her attention to the practical task of bringing each of us a white bucket and a white box of tissue. I pulled myself up on my elbows and watched her slowly tend to her chore as if she were managing a sacred chalice instead of a plastic puke bucket. She got down on one knee, placed the bucket and tissues next to each person, then brought her hands together at her heart and bowed her head. It seemed everything about this night was ceremonial.

The other journeyers had set up photos of gurus, prayer beads, crystals, and other special objects near their mats. One man in the back corner had what appeared to be an entire altar of personal items stacked on a shelf. I had brought a single heart-shaped rock, which I placed next to my pillow. The man in the corner writhed and moaned in front of his altar in agony or ecstasy, I couldn't tell which. But I quickly turned my eyes and ears away from eavesdropping. It was so like me to be a voyeur rather than feel my own experience, and I didn't want that. Not this time. I wanted to be present for whatever came. I stretched out and closed my eyes and remembered the shaman's instruction: *Try to let go and surrender*.

The shaman put down his guitar, picked up a drum, and began drumming a steady hard-soft-soft, hard-soft-soft rhythm. The sound entered my ears and twisted into my imagination like the vines of the ayahuasca plant. The drum resonance shook through my sternum and fired up a tingling sensation in my chest. I felt the drumbeat wrap itself into the deepest core of my being and squeeze tight until I imagined an iridescent green fluid oozing out from between my ribs. That was when I felt the first wave. Rolling over, I sat up and reached for the white bucket. I braced it between my knees, hung my head, and took in slow deep breaths. At the other end of the room, someone was retching and heaving and making growling noises. *Oh God*, I thought, *please don't let that happen to me*. I detested vomiting and hoped it would not be part of my ayahuasca journey, although I'd read that vomiting and diarrhea were a common experience from the medicine.

As my body and mind swirled in a surreal ride, I whispered to Grandmother, "I want an artistic breakthrough, but please be gentle with me and teach me what I need to know without scaring the shit out of me."

I had learned from the shaman that ayahuasca will give generously if you come to it with openness, humility, and respect. An ayahuasca trip can be a journey to the brink of death or to the source of all creation. All I really needed to do was surrender and trust that the ancient medicine knew where she was taking me. Unlike others of my generation, I hadn't done recreational drugs in the sixties. But this was something different; this was a journey with a plant medicine. So there I was at age sixty-eight taking psychedelics for the first time. It felt like a late-in-life rite of passage. Breathe. Focus. Settle. I worked to calm myself and stave off the waves of nausea. But like the thick intertwining vines of the powerful plant itself, I felt my insides clamp down in a corkscrewed twisting that I thought might turn me inside out. And in a way, it did.

A deep grunting roar echoed out into the room, and it took a moment for me to realize it had come from my own throat. I gripped my bucket and gagged. The nausea was so intense I wanted to vomit; I would have welcomed the release. But all I did was gag and spit. The movement started low in my belly, this time all the way down in my womb. I felt a tidal wave of sorrow accompanied by a desperate desire to purge myself of whatever was stuck inside me. I groaned and growled and gagged. I whined and whimpered and wanted to wail, but it didn't come. Quiet tears salted my cheeks. Low moans caught in my throat. I pressed my opened palms to my face, stifling the frightening sounds that emanated from me. Crying was okay, but I held back from freely releasing the tsunami of sound and grief that waited to gush out of me.

Could I find the courage to pull my grief and heartbreak out of the shadows and into the light?

Suddenly the angel assistant in white was there by my side. She placed her hand on my shoulder so lightly I had to look and make sure it was there. She leaned in. "It's okay," she said. "When you let it go, you cry for everyone here. You do us all a great service."

And then, in that moment, everything that had been building up inside of me for years broke loose. I had long suspected that the pent-up sorrow was not mine alone. I sensed it came from a vast field—a collective reservoir of ancestral and planetary grief. The first time I had felt this great sorrow was thirteen years earlier on my wilderness quest in the Inyo National Forest. I had cried and cried during that quest for reasons I couldn't understand or explain. My guide, Anne, had suggested I was crying Mother Earth's tears. I hadn't known what to make of her suggestion at the time. After that quest I became hypersensitive to reading or hearing about environmental devastation. National Public Radio featured news stories about the number of species disappearing from the planet, and I folded over, gut-punched in grief. Maps in a magazine showed the disastrous consequences of global warming, and I crumbled to my knees on the kitchen floor and wept. Sometimes I scream-cried. *What have we done? What will the future be like for our grandchildren and great-grandchildren?*

That night, in the safe hands of the capable shaman and the angel in white, the sorrow that was tied up inside me broke free. I was powerless against the force. Up on all fours, I vomited inexplicable amounts of fluid from a stomach that had taken in next to nothing over the last eight hours, only a few ounces of ayahuasca and sips of water. Bouts of heaving and retching hurled up from all the way down in my toes. Great ragged sobs exploded out of me like a million wounded souls crying for relief. I had cried hard in my life, but never like this. I cried for my two failed marriages and for leaving my children with their father. I wept for the millions of suffering beings around the world. I wailed for mass extinction of species and a planet that's slowly burning up. It was as if my whole body turned inside out, completely emptied itself physically and emotionally, then shook forcefully to get out every last drop of grief.

At times I felt calm and relieved, floating peacefully downstream. Then it started up again, a boat plunging over an unexpected waterfall. After what felt like hours, my head throbbed and my throat burned, and I needed relief. I tucked my legs into a squat, placed both palms on the floor, and tried to lift my body. I wobbled and fell backward. Within seconds the male assistant appeared at my side.

"I want to go outside for a little while," I whispered, my throat hoarse and sore.

The woman lying next to me mumbled something to herself, then laughed. The man on the other side of me tossed and turned on his mat. I needed privacy. I needed Mother Earth. I thought of how easy my wilderness questing had been in comparison to this arduous, exhausting journey. The aide helped me to my feet, then guided me past bodies lying prone in the dark, up the stairs, and out the door onto a deck surrounded by a lush green forest. I breathed in the fresh pine-scented air. No nausea, at least not for the moment.

"I'm okay," I said. "I'd like to stay out here for a while." The assistant bowed and disappeared back through the doorway.

Cool moisture spread over my swollen face and against the soles of my feet and restored me back to center. I held on to the deck railing, pulled air into my grateful lungs, and gazed up into the arboreal canopy. Floodlights from the deck lit up the nighttime forest. Every branch and leaf sparkled with a shimmering silver outline. It was as if I were seeing all the flora—the fern, salal, rhododendron, Douglas fir, cedar, bigleaf and vine maple—for the first time. Every arc and curve of the botanical wonderland was strikingly clear and vivid in a riot of green, yellow, and red foliage. Whispers echoed through the rich green understory. Another swell of nausea rolled through my gut. Off the deck and up the path into the forest, I went to my knees.

"Please," I said to who or whatever entities and energies breathed out there with me. "I am emptied out; I can't take any more. What is it you want from me?"

This time the cacophony of whispers morphed into one clear androgynous voice, a presence. "You have stepped into the river of grief that flows under the surface of everything and everyone," the voice said. I scanned the sea of green searching for the source of the voice, a person, or a vision. Nothing but leaf and limb.

Wind shook the trees and released a shower of raindrops that jeweled like diamonds through the air and shattered into a billion particles of light. I sat mesmerized.

"Don't be afraid to let the river carry you. Let yourself be a matriarch of sorrow," the bodiless presence continued.

I absorbed the words with the feeling—no, more like the deep knowledge—that what I heard was true. It was one of those things you know, but you don't know how you know; you just know. I did feel as if I was being apprenticed as a matriarch of grief and sorrow. I thought back to the wilderness quest all those years ago when I had first connected with deep sadness. I had dipped my toe into the river of grief. For all those years it had stayed under the surface of my consciousness. Now, on the ayahuasca journey, I was fully submerged into a whirlpool of sorrow. I feared I would be carried away into a dark abyss, over the edge of an impossible waterfall with no way back to myself. Crawling across the wet forest duff to a nearby tree, I shifted to my backside and leaned against the massive trunk. The overhead canopy gleamed like emeralds. Sparkling fractals of light collided and shattered into leafy jewels. I saw my heart shatter into the same billion crystals of prismatic lime-colored light.

Kahlil Gibran wrote: "Your joy is your sorrow unmasked, and the self-same well from which your laughter arises was oftentimes filled with your tears. And the deeper that sorrow carves into your being, the more joy you can contain." I had loved this quote for thirty years, and now I felt like I was living the visual manifestation of those words, watching pieces of my heart break off and dance through the drizzling rain.

A surge of wind showered the forest with evergreen needles and the smell of pine. I hugged my arms to my chest and rested my chin on my knees. "I understand," I said to the presence. "I am willing to carry the grief. But I need a lifeline . . . something to hold on to."

The answer eased into me like an apparition through a crack in a door. *Carrying grief means welcoming heartbreak and having faith in deep sorrow. Carrying grief means surrendering into the idea that everything is already broken. And the world becomes more vivid and exquisite because everything is temporary.*

The lifeline I had asked for was not in finding something to hold on to; it was in letting go and courageously riding the waves of sorrow that are part of life. It was antithetical to what I wanted; I wanted all the sadness to go away. But in that moment of communion with the forest and Mother Earth, I knew the answer wasn't to push grief away. The answer was to let grief lead me into what is most alive in me: my art. I needed to take my broken heart and turn it into art. I needed to transform my grief into beauty and keep offering a way for others to do the same.

This was the artistic breakthrough I had asked for—not something new and different but deepening into what I was already doing: midwifing people's experiences in the *kint-sugi* breaking and mending ceremonies. I had been bringing people together in community to break and mend bowls as a metaphor for our broken hearts and our broken earth. My ayahuasca journey was an encouraging push to keep on.

I curled over my knees, bowed down, and let the moss on the forest floor caress my face. I breathed in the earthy smell of mushrooms, lichens, and algae and felt the moist flora against my skin. Then, sopping wet, I started to shiver. It was time to seek shelter. I left the tree and stepped up onto the deck at the same moment the attendant appeared at the door. He took my arm, and we walked back across the threshold into the house. I stood dripping in the foyer while the aide retrieved my bag with clean, dry clothes.

"When you go into the bathroom, it's best not to look in the mirror," he said. "And don't turn on the light; it will hurt your eyes."

I nodded and took my clothes and towel into the small candlelit room. Moving in what felt like slow motion, I stripped down and dried myself, then put on a sweatshirt and a pair of flannel pajama pants. Senses heightened by the drug, every cell in my body welcomed the dryness and warmth. My nausea had completely subsided, and I breathed freely—a welcome relief.

It's best not to look in the mirror, the attendant had said. But why not? What could possibly be worse than what I had already gone through? Curiosity got the best of me. I turned around and peered into the bathroom mirror. Flickering candlelight bounced particles of dancing light over my face and hair. The pleasant picture quickly melted away and was replaced by the image of Green Woman, a witchy pagan goddess face encircled by a corona of leaves with branches and vines sprouting from my mouth and nostrils. The image was intriguing and frighteningly real. I pressed my fingers to my face and felt my skin to be sure I was intact, still myself.

I squeezed my eyes shut, then opened them. My face morphed into a bare white skull with coal-black eye sockets, a gaping hole where the nose had been, the teeth in a permanent grimace. The skull began to shift and turn to allow a view from different angles, like an anatomy lesson. I watched, fascinated by the rounded symmetry of my head and the angular bones of my cheeks. A sadness overtook me. *Death is the ultimate breaking that can't be mended*, I thought. I started to cry, and the haunting skull began crying too—thick blood-red teardrops. Death and I cried together in the mirror in a spectacle of grief and love.

I blinked, and the vision disappeared. My face returned. I didn't wait for another distortion; the death skull was enough. I turned away from the mirror, splashed cold water onto my face, and slipped out the bathroom door, hoping I would remember the vision later when I was out from under the influence of the medicine.

Back on my mat on the basement floor, I crawled under my blanket, spent and relieved. I picked up the heart-shaped stone I had brought and held it close to my chest. The hallucination was why the attendant had warned me not to look in the mirror. But I felt more love and compassion than fear; I had befriended my own death. My ayahuasca journey had brought me to the threshold of grief I had been carrying for myself and for Mother Earth for two decades. On every quest I had fallen more deeply in love with the wilderness. The cells in my body, once a part of Mother Earth, felt the attachment to her womb, like an umbilical cord supplying continuous nourishment. The devastation caused by drought, fire, and melting glaciers that she experienced hurt me too, as if it were happening to my own body, which, in a way, it was.

I left my resistance to feeling grief and sadness out in the lush, wet forest. I was no longer afraid of letting my heart break. Now I would go all in, deepened and ripened by my apprenticeship with sorrow.

HEALING THE MOTHER WOUND: JULY FULL BUCK MOON

*Goodbyes are only for those who love with
their eyes. Because for those who love with heart
and soul there is no such thing as separation.*

—Rumi

My mother died shortly after my thirteenth wilderness quest, under a July full Buck Moon, named by the Algonquin people for the full-grown antlers on male deer that time of year. The quest that year brought healing to the relationship between my mother and me, although she was not there with me—not in person anyway. But I felt her presence on the Modoc land, as if her spirit had already partly left her body. I knew she was dying; she had stopped eating, and hospice had been called in. It was comforting but also disconcerting, like being haunted by someone who had not yet died, a soul lingering in the doorway where the two worlds touched. While the COVID-19 virus swept across the world killing thousands, I was out in a wild place contemplating the imminent death of the person who had given me life.

In a clearing beneath a grand juniper, with views of the rolling sage-covered hills of the chaparral, I set up my chair at the edge of our circle. Along with me at the gathering was my beloved guide, Anne, and seven Wild Hearts sisters. I settled back in my chair and looked around at the others with curiosity. What was each woman's purpose this year? What adventures awaited us on our solo fasting time? It was a familiar ceremony for us, being together at base camp for a couple of days before we struck out on our own on the Modoc land, listening to one another's stories and appreciating the intimate community we had built together.

One by one, each woman shared her quest intention with sincerity and commitment to this ancient ceremony we had practiced together under Anne's guidance for close to a decade. As each woman spoke, I wrote her intention in my journal verbatim. I did this on every quest. Then, during my solo time, I would send a blessing to each quester that her intention be fulfilled. It was my way of staying connected to everyone while I was out there on my own. When it came my turn to share, I picked up the feather and beaded wooden talking stick and leaned forward in my chair. "My mother will die within the next couple of weeks. I want to use this quest to resolve any lingering anger or resentment toward her before she passes. I want to give my full attention and let nature guide me toward healing. I want to welcome everything and push away nothing, even if it's unpleasant or painful."

I stopped and let the gravity of what I had said sink in. I knew I held on to old resentments toward my mother. A therapist once told me we all suffer from a mother wound, whether caused by under-mothering or over-mothering. We all carry scars. Mothering is demanding work, and sometimes, maybe most times, mothers don't get it 100 percent right.

It was easy to blame my mother for my faults and hang-ups, but I also had the choice to heal the most intimate relationship I would ever have. And I had come to my ultimate mother, Mother Nature, for that healing. Anne tilted her head and squinted up into the grandmother tree for a moment, then turned to me. "Are you prepared for the possibility that your mother might die while you are out on your solo time?" she asked.

I looked up into the tree. "I really don't think she will. Something tells me she won't go for another week or two. At least I hope not."

Anne's question got me thinking, though. Had I made the right decision to come on the quest, knowing that my mother was in her last days? I wanted to be at her bedside when her spirit transitioned out of her body, but my annual wilderness quest had become important too, a sacred ceremony I planned for all year. I wanted—needed—to be out on the land with Mother Earth, for strength and renewal. Or was I telling myself all this to avoid being at my mother's bedside when she passed? I wasn't sure which was true. Maybe both. My mother and I had never talked about how she wanted to die, whether she wanted her family with her. "Let's talk about something more pleasant," she'd say whenever my sisters or I brought up the topic.

Did I have the courage to look death squarely in the face again?

Later that day, when we chose our questing spots, I opted to stay closer than usual to base camp in case I needed to leave early. I had left Anne's cell phone number with my sister on Anne's promise that she would go out to the edge of the ridge and check her phone for messages every day. I found a place nestled between evergreen trees on a nearby hillside five hundred yards or so from base camp. The distance between two of the junipers would be wide enough to hang my hammock, and a nearby rock ledge would serve as a shelf for my water jugs and backpack. There was a flat spot in the middle of three trees with a thick, soft layer of duff for my sleeping pad. I remembered the lines of a favorite Mary Oliver poem:

> *I thought the earth remembered me, she/ took me back*
> *so tenderly, arranging/ her dark skirts, her pockets/ full*
> *of lichens and seeds.*

I placed my bag over the familiar forest floor, then lay down and looked out through the trees. From my perfect camp spot, I could see across the chaparral to the comforting sight of the towering Grandmother Juniper and the firepit in the center of camp. And I had a clear view of the three-quarter moon rising over the eastern horizon.

I spent the first day of my solo time stretched out in a purple nylon hammock hung in the shade between two tall junipers. I dropped my leg over the side, and when the hammock stopped rocking, I dug my bare foot into the forest duff to restart the motion. The warm breeze rattled through the tall grass of the chaparral like small dry bones. The movement of air was a welcome relief from the searing afternoon sun. Sips of water helped dissipate the metallic taste of toxins burning out of my body from fasting. Lying in my hammock, rocking between the two junipers, I wondered if my mother was still alive, and if I might feel something when she passed. I pulled my journal out from where I'd tucked it beside me in the hammock and started writing a letter.

Dear Mom . . . Remember the time . . . I never understood . . . Why did you . . . Why didn't you . . . and on and on. Questions that would never be answered, like, *Why didn't you talk to me about birth control when you knew I was having sex at fourteen?*

The day I told my mother I was pregnant, she pulled her robe close to her chest and sat mute on her side of the couch. I perched on the other end with my arms crossed over my cotton T-shirt. Her eyes widened, squinted, and bore down on me. Then her face softened, and her head tilted to the side.

"Who is the father?" she asked.

"Bob," I snapped back. Did she think I was sleeping with other guys?

"What are you going to do?" she asked. What was *I* going to do, like it was my problem for me to solve on my own. I bit my lip and started to cry.

"We're going to get married," I said. My answer made my mother cry too.

There we sat, my mother at one end of the couch and me at the other, crying alone together. Both of us disappointed. Both of us ashamed for our own reasons. I wanted her to come over to me and put her arms around me and tell me everything would be okay. I felt stranded. But later that year, when I went into labor, she would be right there beside me, holding my hand and offering encouragement.

I gave my full attention to memories of my mother that day and wrote in my journal for what seemed like hours. After a time, my head ached, my eyes burned, and I needed a break. I slipped from the hammock, put on my day pack, and headed out for a hike.

Sunlit clouds drifted across a clear blue sky. Pumice dirt crunched underfoot as I ventured west toward the sun. In the distance, white shapes scattered over the ground caught my eye. Curious, I picked up my pace. Closer, I recognized the bleached-out bones of an animal carcass: leg bones, hip bones, vertebrae, and ribs. The size and length of the leg bones appeared to be from a deer. But no skull. The skull was missing, most likely dragged away by an animal. Or a hunter had cut off the head for a trophy rack of horns, then thrown the carcass aside. The bones had been picked clean, no sign of the fur, muscle, and sinew that once made up the body of the deer. I stooped down, picked up a rib bone, and instinctively raised it to my nose. It smelled like everything else on the chaparral, like dirt and sage with a hint of juniper. *This is what it all comes down to*, I thought, *a scattering of bones in the dirt.*

The wind picked up, blew across the canyon, and created a dust tornado that danced like a spirit in the distance. Wind on a wilderness quest was a sign that things were being stirred up. I thought of Thawte, the wind spirit in Lakota mythology who guides one through obstacles. *Pick up the bones*, she whispered. I collected the remains, then laid the bones out to recreate the original rib cage, seven on one side but only six on the other. I scanned the area for another bone to even out the number, but it had either been eaten or carried away. Another gust of wind stirred up a dust funnel nearby, and I pulled my collar up over my face.

It was auspicious, finding thirteen bones on my thirteenth wilderness quest. There are thirteen full moons in a calendar year, one for each of the months plus the blue moon when there are two full moons in one month. The number thirteen links with the idea of transformation and shows up when we are about to go through something that is difficult and painful, but also promises that the metamorphosis is necessary. In the Tarot deck, thirteen is linked with the death card and tells us to prepare for a momentous change.

I tucked the thirteen ribs into my day pack and headed back to my questing place. Once there, I got down on my knees. Rocks dug into my skin as I arranged the ribs on a flat rocky outcropping that jutted out from the side of the hill. The natural stone shelf made the ideal place for my altar of a gourd rattle, juniper berries, two blue-gray feathers, a small bouquet of yellow buckwheat flowers, a fully intact snakeskin I'd found earlier, and the rib bones. I arranged and rearranged the bones. First in a row, then in a circle. I settled on a sunburst pattern to create a radiating effect. The altar felt complete and ready for a ceremonial goodbye.

There are hundreds of ways to tie up unfinished business and say goodbye to a loved one. For me there is none more powerful than the death lodge ceremony—an act of completion for unfinished business. I had performed death lodge ceremonies on past quests—for ex-husbands, old bosses, and friends. People I had hurt. People who had hurt me. I'd created death lodges in cave-like recesses under rocks and bushes or made circles out in the open from whatever I found on the forest floor. A death lodge could be anywhere. In my earlier death lodges, the ritual followed a pattern: I stepped across the threshold, shook my rattle, and invited someone in. Then someone appeared from my subconscious and stepped into the lodge. I told them everything on my mind and listened to what they said. Then the next person came in and spoke, then the next one, over and over until the ceremony felt complete. Past death lodge ceremonies had lasted for an hour, two at the most.

The death lodge ceremony for my mother was different from any I'd done in the past. I drew a simple circle in the dirt next to my altar and stood at the symbolic entry point. "I am GG, and this is my death lodge. May my heart be open to any who enter here." Three black turkey vultures circled overhead, as if on cue. Stepping into the death lodge, I sat on a rock, closed my eyes, and shook a gourd rattle that my mother had given me as a gift, a black lizard painted on its surface. I rattled standing, pacing, and sitting. I rattled until my backside started to go numb. I was ready to call it quits when, behind my closed eyes, my maternal lineage appeared—my mother, grandmother, and great-grandmother. My mother came in beautiful and young, as in a photograph I had of her from 1940, with her hourglass figure and wavy dark hair, looking straight at the camera. Sitting on her left and holding her hand was her mother, Ruth. And on her right, holding her other hand, was her grandmother Maude. We sat together in silence for a while, and then my mother started to speak. She told me about growing up in poverty on her grandparents' farm. She shared the heartbreak of seeing her mentally ill mother hammer magazine pictures to walls with roofing nails, and the sting of being scrubbed raw with powdered soap in a washtub. She talked about the stress and toil of teaching school full-time while raising children, being the main bread winner in the family, and the chaos of living with an alcoholic husband. She said that, in order to keep forging ahead with what needed to be done, she had closed off her emotions. I had heard some of these things before, but never like this. This time we weren't mother and child; we were woman and woman, listening and sharing our truths without any blame or judgment. Ruth and Maude sat like steadfast bookends on either side of my mother and said nothing.

I shared my story with my mother. I told her that, as a child, I had tried to stay quiet and unobtrusive so I didn't give her any reason to be more upset than she already was. We were totally open and honest with one another—she apologized for her shortcomings, and I expressed how conflicted I felt about my relationship with her, my deep love for and intense frustration with her. I went all in and gave the death lodge experience with my mother my full presence for as long as it took to get it all out. I thanked Ruth and Maude for giving us life and for their courage and strength. Then the four of us sat together without speaking for a while. I felt at peace.

When the ceremony was over, I wiped my eyes, blew my nose, and declared the death lodge closed. I stepped out of the circle I'd drawn in the dirt and crawled back into the comfort of my hammock. My mother's presence stayed with me during the rest of my fast in what turned out to be a four-day-long death lodge. Images of her life flashed through my consciousness like a cinematic feature. Some memories were familiar from photos or stories she had told me, while others were new, and I wondered where they had come from. Were they from my own imagination, or had her memories somehow merged into my consciousness from the death lodge experience?

One afternoon when I was five or six, I came in the front door crying. The neighborhood kids had been teasing me about my brown saddle shoes. I went to my mother, who sat on the couch, head down, red pencil in hand, grading papers.

"They're all laughing at me," I said through my sobs. She didn't look up. "Just ignore them." Her hand continued down the page.

I ran out to the backyard fishpond, sat down in the moss by the water, and cried. I took the ugly, clunky shoes off and lowered my feet into the cold green water. A group of koi goldfish gathered and hovered in a familiar routine, watching and wary but not concerned enough to swim away. I held still. The orange, exotic, fan-tailed creatures approached, nibbled at a toe, then darted back under lily pads. I concentrated hard to keep from curling my toes and scaring them away. I kept my feet in the water until my skin got too cold to feel the fish kisses.

The accumulation of small incidences over the years and my mother's stoic approach to any emotion taught me not to expect comfort from her. Instead, I learned to find it in places like the fishpond in the backyard and the ravine across the street.

Two smooth-feathered gray mourning doves flew over my hammock and landed in a nearby tree. One cooed a lonesome lament; the other moved closer to it, and their bodies met. Through the years, whenever my mother hugged me, I froze a little inside and waited for it to be over. I hugged her back halfheartedly, but I never opened my arms to her. I kept that wall up throughout my life. I was a good daughter on the outside, visiting her often, taking care of her after breast cancer surgery, and calling her every Sunday. But inside, a part of me stayed bone dry toward her. Lying there watching the doves, I realized my mother wasn't the only one who had withheld affection.

Over the last twenty-five years, I'd kept all the cards I'd received from her for birthdays, Christmas, and Valentine's Day. Before the quest, knowing my mother was fading, I had sorted through the cards and pulled out all fifty-one of them, most of which she had hand painted. In every card, without exception, she wrote that she loved me, how proud she was of me, and that I had brought joy to her life. What she couldn't show or tell me in person, she had written in those cards. What I couldn't tell her in person, I'd spoken in the death lodge and written in my journal.

A small red-breasted nuthatch landed in the juniper and hopped upside down along the tree trunk. As it bounced along, the little bird poked its tiny beak into the recesses of the layered bark. Those layers of bark offer protection for the inside tender parts of the tree. I had put a thick layer around my heart and decided not to let myself want love and affection from my mother. With cues from nature and uninterrupted time for reflection, I was picking away at what had been hidden inside me. The wall was crumbling. Love and affection are a two-way street.

That afternoon, I finished the letter in a few short lines.

Dear Mom, I'm sorry. Please forgive me. I forgive you.
Thank you for giving me life. Thank you for loving me.
I love you. Goodbye.

The next day, I gathered up the gourd rattle, feathers, snakeskin, and thirteen rib bones, wrapped them in a handkerchief, and tucked them into my backpack before I headed back to base camp. The two doves landed in the top of the juniper and cooed back and forth, their soft drawn-out calls like a comforting lament, *Coo—ooo, oo-oo-oo.*

Throughout the days of my quest, I had spoken to my mother, sung to her, reminisced with her, written her a long letter, cried with her, and hiked with her over the sage-covered hills of the Modoc wilderness. In an inexplicable way, my mother's spirit met mine out there in the wild under the waxing moon, where I had no distractions, and she had no limits. "Out beyond ideas of wrongdoing and right doing there is a field," Rumi wrote. "I'll meet you there. When the soul lies down in that grass the world is too full to talk about." My time on Mother Earth reopened my heart and prepared me for the last moments I had with my mother.

July 6, 2020, was gray and dreary, one of those days when the sky gave no sign of what time it was. It was the kind of weather that made the redwood trees thrive on the Northern California coast—overcast, foggy, and drizzling. It had been sunny and warm for the previous seven days, but on that Monday, the Humboldt Bay marine layer brought a thick salt- and seaweed-scented gloom to the air.

With my jacket hood pulled up tightly over my head against the damp, I shoved my hands in my pockets and set out on my usual walking route through the small-town neighborhood playground and past rows of tidy one-story cottages with colorful flower gardens. I was headed downtown to the Arcata Plaza, the same destination as every other morning since I'd arrived at my sister's house a week earlier. My mother's death was imminent, and the daily walk freed me from the constant vigilance and the waiting. At one point, we thought she was dying, but then her two friends came to visit, and she rallied and joined us at the lunch table. She was unconscious most of the time, but now and then she would surprise us with funny comments about seeing wings and halos sprouting from her angel caregivers (us) or telling us to stop arguing about how best to take care of her because she wasn't planning on giving out any prizes.

"Your sisters and your ex-husbands are all waiting for you in heaven, Mom," Dea said while we were moving Mom farther up in the bed.

"Well, let's not get too carried away," Mom said, with a sarcastic tone. We laughed much harder than the comment warranted because the release felt so good.

A group of raucous crows gathered at the corner of the street, hopping around making growling and scolding sounds. In the gutter, they picked at a small furry lump, a decaying squirrel carcass. As I approached, the crows scattered and flew away. One long blue-black feather drifted onto the sidewalk. I picked it up to add to my collection at home and continued toward town. Twenty minutes from my sister's house, past the grocery store and in front of the local bank, my phone chimed. "Come back home," my sister texted. "It's happening."

I pivoted around and raced back up the hill, blinking furiously to hold back the emotion that teetered at the edge of my heart. I had known this day would come, and I'd thought about how I would react, whether I would fall apart or be stoic and hold it all in. Now I knew. I stopped breathing for a moment. My heart pounded in my chest, and my vision went white.

A short distance up the incline, I was breathless and knew I couldn't run fast enough to make it to my sister's house in time. I scanned the busy street for someone I could ask for a ride, someone who looked safe. Ahead at the curb, a young woman opened the door of a blue sedan and ducked in, but she started the engine and drove away before I reached her. Cars roared up the street. I considered the possibility of flagging someone down, but they might mistake me for some sort of lunatic. Arcata was a small, quaint town, but it had its share of drug addicts and transients. Locals were wary.

At the top of the hill was a parking lot scattered with cars. I checked the driver seats for a single woman at the wheel. They were empty except for a tattered white pickup truck parked directly in front of me. The truck door opened, and a bearded man with a tangle of dark hair leaned out.

"Are you okay, ma'am?" he asked. I sized him up: concerned expression, working clothes, and a kind tone in his voice. *It's not the time to be choosy about a ride*, I thought.

"Can you give me a ride? It's just five minutes from here," I said. "My mother is dying." My voice cracked. Tears burned.

"Sure. Get in," he said.

I tugged the passenger door open and slid into the cab next to a pair of work gloves and a hard hat. Food wrappers and empty coffee cups littered the floor.

"My sister lives on Eye Street," I said.

"I know Eye Street," he said. "I do maintenance work on apartments down there." He pulled out onto the street and headed north, the diesel motor clattering through the foggy air. "Can I say a prayer for your mother?"

"Yes, that would be nice," I said, my hands clenched in my lap.

"What's her name?" he asked, turning his head from side to side to check for oncoming traffic as he rolled through a stop sign.

"Dodie."

"Lord, we pray for Dodie and her family. May you welcome her and hold her in your light. Amen."

"Amen," I said, relieved at the sincerity of the prayer as well as the brevity. I was trying to hold my emotions at bay and didn't want to hear a lengthy sermon from a stranger while my mother lay dying.

The man dropped me off at the house and I said a quick thank-you. I charged through the front door, threw my jacket on a chair, and headed into the bedroom. Lea sat in the brown leather easy chair next to the bed, her gray hair pulled back, her eyes red and swollen, her hands folded in her lap. Dea, Lea's twin, perched on the closed commode, the only other chair in the room. She had the same watery red eyes, and her hands tilted up and down in rhythm as she knitted.

"She's gone to be with God," Dea said.

A hint of burned sage lingered in the air from the energy cleansings I had performed for my mother in her last days. High on the wall above the bed hung a row of silk-screened prayer flags with Native symbols. On the opposite wall hung an elk-skin drum. Around the room we had placed all my mother's favorite paintings. On the windowsill next to her bed, a white candle flickered. We had kept one burning there for the last several days. A huge bouquet of white lilies, roses, and chrysanthemums surrounded by green foliage graced the dresser. And in the bed lay my mother, white as the lilies.

All my life I had seen my mother in various forms of moving, breathing, and living. Even when she was sick or sleeping, life radiated from her skin and hair, from her eyes and face. But now she lay still—beyond still, an empty shell. Her thick white hair spread over the pillow like a halo around her head. Her chin dropped to the side, and her jaw slacked open. Her spirit was gone.

I stepped to the window and slid it farther open so her soul could pass through and rise up to heaven, a tradition I'd read about somewhere.

"She died about five minutes ago," Lea said. "I was here when it happened. She just stopped breathing. It was peaceful. She just . . . went."

A terrible ache rolled in my chest. I had wanted to be there when my mother passed. I remembered my friend Judith, a hospice chaplain, had told me that sometimes people wait until everyone leaves the room to die, or they die with everyone gathered around them. People die when the time is right for them. She had warned me not to be surprised if I wasn't in the room when my mother passed. It was not for me to decide. Still, I couldn't help but regret that I'd gone for a walk that morning.

My mother's blue-veined hands crossed over her chest, and I placed my hand on her forehead. "She's still warm," I said, studying her face, the place under her cheeks where skin caved into bone, the skeleton of her collarbone and ribs, each one protruding under her thin nightgown. I lingered in the last warmth of her body.

"It's okay, Mom," I said, though I knew she could no longer hear me. "We're here. Don't be afraid. We love you."

The three of us stayed with our mother for a long time, until the room closed in on us and we needed a reprieve from the intensity of her deathbed. We lit more candles and placed them around the room. Then we retreated to the living room and replayed the events of the last days—her moment of death and all that had happened. Talking about it eased our sadness, reassured us that we had done the right things for her in her last days. I have always loved my two older sisters, but never more than in those moments following my mother's death.

After a time, I returned to my mother's bedside. Her eye sockets were beginning to sink, and her pale skin was sallow and pallid. Studying the changes death brought to her body, I felt that more was needed to sanctify my mother's passing. I mentioned to my sisters that perhaps we might wash her body. But they didn't think Mom would have liked that, and I couldn't argue with them. But I wanted a ritual, something beautiful to honor her.

I slipped out the front door, walked down the steps, and stood in front of a six-foot hydrangea bush that grew next to the house. I picked thirteen apple-sized periwinkle blossoms and carried them to the bedroom. I laid the bouquet on her chest, then lifted my mother's head, gathered her thick snow-white hair, and tucked it back. I placed the billowing blossoms in a circle around her head. White pillow, white hair, white skin, and a halo of delicate lavender-blue blossoms. I felt grace slip through me like a silky veil. In those last moments, any anger and resentment I had for anything my mother had ever done or not done vanished, leaving nothing but unconditional love.

I stood back and took in the scene. This would be my last memory of her—her lying on her deathbed surrounded by flowers like a sacred maternal icon.

"I love you, Mom," I said, then sat down next to the bed and wept.

BLESSINGS FOR BABY BATS

*If the world is to be healed through human efforts, I
am convinced it will be by ordinary people; people whose
love for this life is even greater than their fear; people
who can open to the web of life that called us into being.*
—Joanna Macy

My two great-granddaughters and I sat together
at the foot of a red cedar tree that stood in the middle
of a freshly mowed green lawn. A homeschool nature lesson
pamphlet and a box of colored pencils lay on the ground
beside us. Nora, six years old, and Caroline, three, shared
their mother's beauty—heart-shaped faces, rich dark hair,
and so-dark-brown-they-looked-black eyes. Jack, the girls'
seven-year-old brother, was at school that morning. So it was
just the two girls and me. The red cedar we gathered under
was in the front yard of their grandparents' home: my son,
Bill, and daughter-in-law (I called her my daughter-in-love),
Rachel. It was October, and I had come to Maryland for a

visit and to celebrate my seventieth birthday with my East Coast family. Four generations together.

My granddaughter Megan, pregnant with her fourth child, had asked me to watch the girls and teach their nature lesson while she attended a prenatal appointment. Keeping a three- and five-year-old focused on a lesson was challenging, but I had become skilled at redirecting children's attention from my experience taking care of my Oregon grandchildren, Thea and Silas.

"Okay," I said to the girls. "Here is the next question from the lesson about our tree: How does the bark of the tree smell?"

Nora jumped to her feet and pushed her nose into a pleated fold of the cinnamon-colored bark. Caroline popped up and followed Nora's lead.

"It smells like dirt," Nora said.

"It smells like dirt," Caroline said, echoing her big sister.

"Perfect. Okay. Let's write that down. The red cedar tree bark smells like dirt." I took a sniff of the tree myself, and it did smell like dirt, along with cedarwood overtones. I wrote the girls' responses on the page and moved to the next question.

"What do you hear in the tree?" I asked. But I had lost their attention. The girls had found a daddy longlegs spider and were enthralled. Without any hesitation or trepidation, Nora picked up the spider and held it in her palm. The arachnid moved its long, arched, articulated legs across the skin of her hand, its tiny pill-sized midsection floating along in the center. Caroline watched, so close to her sister's hand that the spider could have reached out a leg and touched her on the nose. I wished I had my camera to capture Caroline's wonder-filled expression.

"Do you always pick up spiders?" I asked, concerned because of brown recluses, black widows, and other poisonous species. I didn't want to stifle the girls' enthusiasm for nature's creatures, but I wanted to be sure they weren't randomly picking up dangerous insects.

"No," said Nora. "But Mom said it's okay to pick up daddy longlegs because they don't bite."

"Yeah, it's a daddy longlegs, and they don't bite," Caroline said with extra emphasis on the "don't bite."

"Maybe you can put the daddy longlegs in the cedar tree, and we'll see what it does."

Nora moved her hand to the tree and held it against the trunk. The spider crawled off her palm and onto the tree, where it immediately disappeared into one of the deep recesses of the cedar bark.

"Uh-oh," I said. "It's gone now."

"That's okay," Nora said. "It can hide in the tree. It will be safe there." Sweet little Nora, always so considerate.

Caroline plopped down in my lap. "Grama GG," she said. "I have to tell you something."

"What do you have to tell me?" I tilted my head and brought my ear down close to her. Caroline whispered a long murmur of incomprehensible syllables into my ear. Then she pulled her head back and looked at me with an impish smile on her rosebud lips. Her pure innocence and beauty gave me such a pain in my heart that I couldn't tell if I was happy or sad.

It was a whisper game. I leaned over and cupped my hand to Caroline's ear and did the same. Then Nora joined in, and we took turns whispering sweet nothings into one another's ears, the girls giggling between the secrets.

"Why don't you whisper to the tree, Caroline, and see if it answers you back," I said.

"Grama GG," she said, with a grown-up impatient tone in her voice, "trees don't have ears."

I chuckled at her sincerity and intention to set me straight. "That's true," I said. "But maybe trees hear us without ears."

Caroline pinched her eyebrows into a frown and looked at me, then looked up at the tree, considering the idea. I widened my eyes, dipped my chin, and smiled at her, hoping I'd planted the suggestion of tree consciousness into her young mind.

I got the girls to refocus on the lesson, and we wrote down what we heard in the tree (birds and wind), the colors of the tree (green and brown), and how the tree felt (scratchy and prickly). I asked the girls to thank the tree for the lesson, and we all gave the big red cedar a hug. Then we walked across the lawn, past the garden, and out to the edge of the woods to the chicken coop.

White leghorns, Rhode Island reds, and speckled Plymouth Rocks strolled through the chicken yard, pecking at the ground and making *bok-bok* sounds. "Let's count the chickens and make sure they are all here," I said.

"One, two, three . . ." The girls counted in unison— eleven chickens. I gave Nora and Caroline each a bucket of cracked corn, and they pitched handfuls through the chicken-wire fence into the pen. To the girls' delight, the chickens clucked and scurried around gobbling up the bits of yellow. I stood back, relishing the sight of little fists dipping into the buckets and the girls walking along the cage line spreading corn, making sure all the chickens were fed.

A long time ago—close to fifty years—I spent time in nature as a young mother with my children, camping, hiking, swimming, and exploring. Back then I took nature for granted. I didn't think twice about the abundance of intriguing species to watch, pure flowing mountain streams to wade in, frogs and snakes to catch and release. My heart tightened in a nostalgic embrace. But the nostalgia morphed into a gut-clench when I thought about what the world might be like when the girls reached my age.

What trees, plants, insects, and animals would they experience in a future climate-changed world? Would they wake up to a red, yellow, and black western tanager hopping on a branch over their heads? Or spend a night out on the chaparral in the company of feral horses watching over them, or sleep with pack rats dropping seeds and twigs onto their faces? Would they see snow-covered mountain peaks or hear the spine-tingling howl of a wolf in the wild?

Watching Nora and Caroline engage with the tree, the spider, and the chickens, I put a prayer out to the universe that my grandchildren, Megan, Thea, and Silas, and my great-grandchildren, Jack, Nora, Caroline, and new baby Molly, might follow my lead: that they would go out into the wilderness alone and find the beauty and surprises that awaited them there—perhaps find themselves there too. I prayed there might still be wild places for them to visit in seventy years.

We have heard it a hundred times: humans are causing the unraveling of life species and ecosystems. As a species, we have overused and under-loved our planetary home. The result is an unhinging of life on Earth as we know it. We are like cells in a living body that is being traumatized, so of course we feel immense grief and sadness about this devastating loss. Grief arises from our profound caring, deep love, and interconnectedness with all life.

It was wilderness questing in the wild—isolation, exposure, and prayer—that helped me understand and experience this interconnectedness with all of Earth's beings. Before I started questing, I was a happy and successful person. I was financially secure, had lots of friends, and had a good relationship with my family. But I felt a longing for deeper connection to something greater than myself. Through wilderness questing and the extraordinary generosity of nature, I found that connection. I went to the land and watched and listened for signs and omens. I opened myself to lessons and guidance from Mother Earth, Gaia, Pachamama, the Great Mother, and supplicated myself to her wisdom. I took the lessons she offered and made peace with my body, rediscovered my childhood passions, and found my life purpose as an artist and teacher. I learned to be comfortable alone and confident in my ability to survive in the wild. I faced my fears and connected with my own wild nature. In the lap of the Great Mother, I forgave myself and others and healed mother wounds—wounds from my mothering and wounds from how I was mothered.

The earth has adapted and survived for 4.5 billion years. She is powerful and patient. We are the offspring of an extraordinarily creative, bountiful mother. She will surely teach us a thing or two about survival over the long term if we listen.

Joanna Macy, author and a beloved mentor, once said: "The greatest gift we can give our world is our full presence, and our choice moment by moment to be present, to stay open." She talks about what an amazing time it is to be alive and have the chance to find out what we have inside us in terms of vitality, alertness, and courage. And that is what wilderness questing brought me—the chance to test my vitality and courage, the chance to fall in love with what is.

Joanna Macy's guidance and wisdom gives me hope. We are waking up. The question is, will enough of us wake up in time to do what is needed to save ourselves?

I want my progeny to know that, in the middle of global warming and species extinction, I tried making a difference the best way I knew how: by falling more deeply in love with what was still here, bearing witness to the indescribable beauty of this world, and encouraging others to do the same through art and ceremony. Bearing witness is not a passive act. It is an act of deep love, especially when you are watching what you love wither away.

I have not turned my back on my sorrow. I have not averted my gaze, nor have I walked away. I have stayed with Mother Earth as I would at the bedside of a dying loved one, holding her, crying with her, and loving her while many of her species' children breathed their last breath. I hold faith that Earth will survive long after we are gone, but it will be a vastly changed place. My prayer is that, before it's too late, we humans will realize that, by saving wild places, we are saving ourselves.

Nature lesson completed and chickens fed, the girls and I moved on to our next adventure: swinging in a hammock at the edge of the lawn between two ironwood trees. Nora and Caroline stood on either side of me, watching with anticipation as if they were in line for a carnival ride, their dark eyes shining.

"Can we get in?" Nora asked.

"Sure," I said. "Hold on, sit down, then bring your legs up so you don't fall out the other side."

With one child at each end, their feet toward the center, I rocked my great-granddaughters back and forth while they giggled with glee. "Let's pretend you are baby bats," I said. "Pull the sides of the hammock over your face and body and hold the sides tight." I showed the girls how to wrap themselves and hold the edges of the canvas together in the center so their bodies were covered and only their sweet faces peeked out from the middle.

"Now close your bat wings and hold them tight until it gets dark," I said. "Bats sleep in the daytime and fly at night." The girls peeked out from their bat-winged cocoons, loving every minute of the game.

"Squeak like little bats, *eeee—eeee—eeee*," I said. The girls started high-pitched squeaking in delighted unison. Their squeaks came out in an octave high enough to mimic real bats, though I doubted they'd ever heard them.

"Grandma GG," Nora said. "You be the grandma bat that rocks us to sleep."

"Good idea," I said. "But before I do that, let's thank the ironwood trees for holding up the hammock for us—thank you, trees."

"Thank you, treeees," the girls chorused.

"Okay, hold on, here we go." I swung the girls in the hammock and felt a warm rush of gratitude for that moment— outside with my great-granddaughters at the edge of the woods, a golden glow of late-afternoon sun shining across the lawn, and the air filled with birdsong and children's laughter. It was a moment I hoped I would remember on my deathbed.

"Rock-a-bye baby bats on the treetop. When the wind blows the cradle will rock . . ."

This was what it had all been for. This was the reason I went out into the wilderness to fast and pray and find my medicine name: Earth Warrior Grandma. This is the reason I go out every year. For myself, for my beloveds, and for our earth.

The girls swayed back and forth, peering out of their bat wings with wide smiles. With my heart overflowing, I sang and rocked my great-granddaughters and whispered a prayer:

Great Spirit: May future generations forgive us our transgressions and learn to live in kinship with all beings on planet Earth. Amen. A-ho. Blessed be.

ACKNOWLEDGMENTS

I owe deep gratitude to the beautiful lands that held me and remembered me on my quests: Death Valley, the Inyo, the North Cascades, and the Modoc. I give thanks to the Grandmother Juniper tree that sheltered my fellow questers and me at our base camp on the Modoc land for years. I give thanks to the fir, cedar, pine, hemlock, juniper, and mahogany trees that provided shade from the sun and shelter from the wind, and the rocks that kept me grounded and gave me places to sit and contemplate. I give thanks to Mother Earth for her ceaseless generosity of resources and to Father Sky for starlit nights. I give thanks to Brother Sun for warming me on those frigid days out alone in the wild and to Sister Moon for lighting my way in the dark. Thank you, Great Spirit, for looking after me and bringing me what I needed on each of my quests.

Thank you to my questing guides, mentors, writing teachers, and writing community:

Anne Stine: for teaching me what it means to be a daughter of Mother Earth.

My Wild Hearts sisters—Cara Walsh, Holly Hertel, Kaya Hagen, Bennie Sullivan, Pat Righter, Paula Backus, and Susanne Peterman: for listening deeply and teaching me to trust myself and others.

Ann Linnea: for her vast wilderness expertise and for teaching me how to greet a tree.

Christina Baldwin: for teaching me the power of story and showing me what is possible.

Deborah Greene-Jacobi: for listening and loving.

Susan Hagen: for understanding my stories and patiently showing me how to improve them.

Ellen Santasiero: for helping me turn my stories into a book.

My sensitivity reader—Savannah Tenderfoot with Salt & Sage Books.

My writing circle companions—Allan Siegel, Cathryn Vogeley, Christine Dreier, Elyse Garrett, John Lucas, Myrna Gusdorf, Cynthia Herron, Eileen Sakai, and Sharon Roemmel: for all your encouragement and brilliant suggestions.

My dear friend Linda West: for listening and supporting me every step of the way.

ABOUT THE AUTHOR

As an artist, art doula, SoulCollage® facilitator, writer, and convener of ceremony, Glenda Goodrich ("GG") brings together earth-based rituals, community gatherings, and creative expression in a search for new ways to show love for the earth. She feels most alive creating art, exploring wild places, and spending time with her two children, three grandchildren, and four great-grandchildren. GG lives in a cottage in the Willamette Valley, Oregon.

Author photo © Benjamin Mah

SELECTED TITLES FROM SHE WRITES PRESS

She Writes Press is an independent publishing company founded to serve women writers everywhere. Visit us at www.shewritespress.com.

Sandwiched: A Memoir of Holding on and Letting Go by Laurie James. $16.95, 978-1-63152-785-2. After her mother has a heart attack and her husband's lawyer delivers some shocking news, James finds herself sandwiched between caring for her parents, managing caregivers, raising four daughters, and trying to understand her husband's choices—so, to keep herself afloat, she seeks therapy, practices yoga, rediscovers nature, and begins to write. Will it be enough to keep her family together?

48 Peaks: Hiking and Healing in the White Mountains by Cheryl Suchors. 978-1-63152-473-8. At forty-eight years old, Cheryl Suchors vows to summit the highest forty-eight peaks in New Hampshire's challenging White Mountains—and discovers, in the years that follow, that in order to feel truly successful, she will have to do much more than tick off peaks.

Amazon Wisdom Keeper: A Psychologist's Memoir of Spiritual Awakening, Loraine Y. Van Tuyl, PhD. $16.95, 978-1-63152-316-8. Van Tuyl, a graduate psychology student and budding shamanic healer, is blindsided when she begins to experience startling visions, hear elusive drumming, and become aware of her inseverable, mystical ties to the Amazon rainforest of her native Suriname. Is she in the wrong field, or did her childhood dreams, imaginary guides, and premonitions somehow prepare her for these challenges?

Be Healthy with Yin Yoga: The Gentle Way to Free Your Body of Everyday Ailments and Emotional Stresses by Stefanie Arend. $18.95, 978-1-63152-590-2. Best-selling author Stefanie Arend puts together many Yin yoga sequences to activate the self-healing powers of body and mind. Replete with high-quality pictures that make the poses and sequences easy to follow and understand, this book is a wonderful support for anyone who wants to take their health back into their own hands.

Sacred & Delicious: A Modern Ayurvedic Cookbook by Lisa Joy Mitchell. $28.95, 978-1-63152-347-2. Both a cookbook and food memoir, this book gives down-to-earth information and instructions for cooking tasty and healing Ayurvedic dishes, celebrating the healing power of food and spices andembodying ancient Ayurvedic wisdom while appealing to a modern
American palate and dietary needs.

The Art of Play: Igniting Your Imagination to Unlock Insight, Healing, and Joy by Joan Stanford. $19.95, 978-1-63152-030-3. Lifelong "non-artist" Joan Stanford shares the creative process that led her to insight and healing, and shares ways for others to do the same.